Building Tradition

10⁰⁰
33453

AF478499

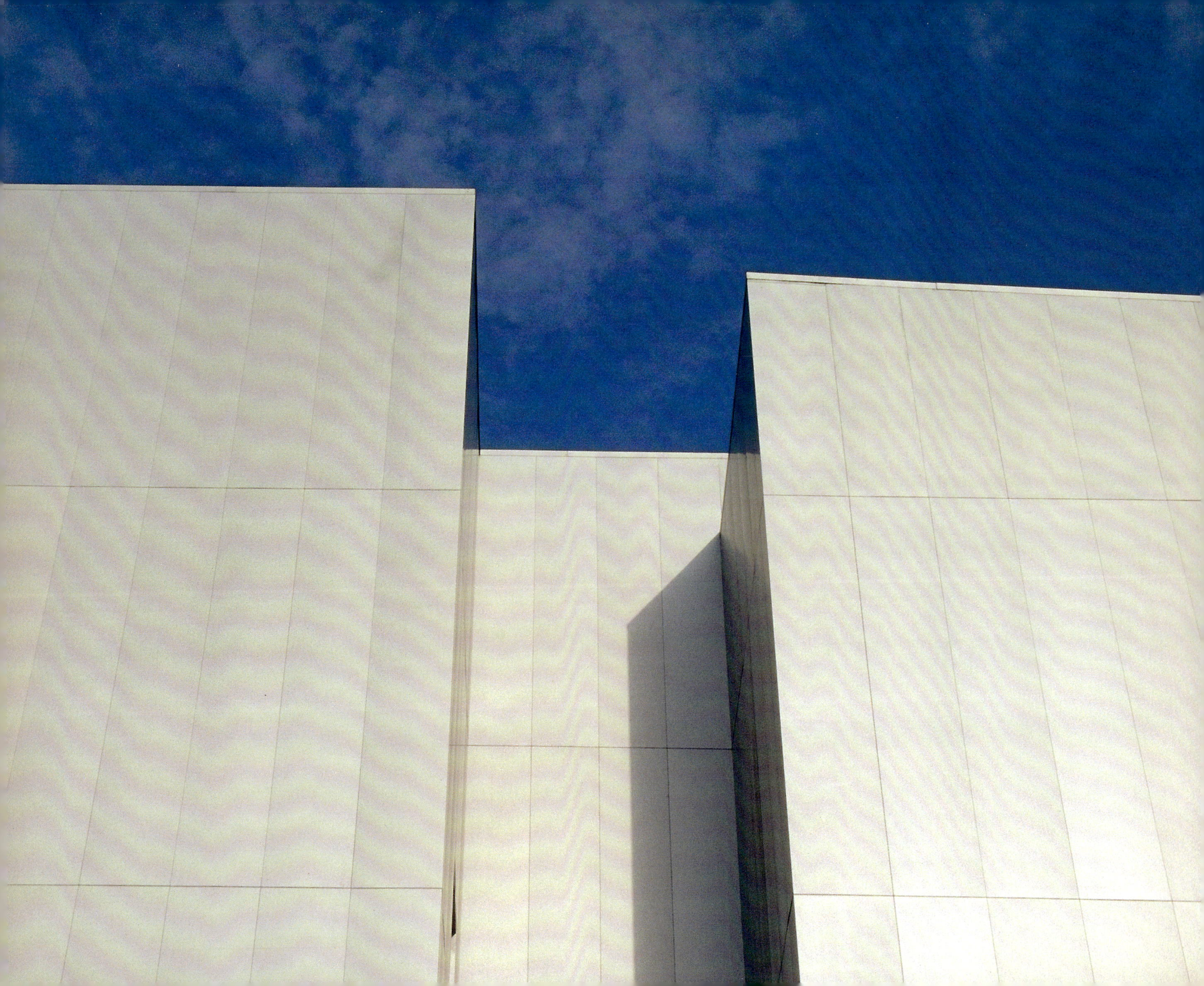

ESSAYS BY **IVAN DOIG** AND **ROCK HUSHKA** AND **PATRICIA MCDONNELL**

DIRECTOR'S FOREWORD BY **JANEANNE A. UPP**

Building Tradition

GIFTS IN HONOR OF THE NORTHWEST ART COLLECTION

TACOMA ART MUSEUM TACOMA, WASHINGTON

Published in conjunction with the opening of the museum's new building at 1701 Pacific Avenue, Tacoma, Washington, and a four-part inaugural exhibition:

    May 3–October 5, 2003
    October 11, 2003–March 21, 2004
    March 27–July 18, 2004
    July 24–December 5, 2004

Exhibition support is generously provided by Key Foundation—a foundation funded by KeyBank. Additional support for the catalogue has been provided by Marquand Books.

Copyright © 2003 Tacoma Art Museum; "Edgewise in Nature" essay copyright © Ivan Doig.
All rights reserved. No part of this publication may be reproduced or transmitted in any form or by any means without prior written permission from the publisher.

ISBN: 0-924335-24-6

Tacoma Art Museum
1701 Pacific Avenue
Tacoma, Washington 98402
www.TacomaArtMuseum.org

Edited by Jana Stone
Proofread by Carrie Wicks
Designed by John Hubbard
Typeset by Jennifer Sugden
Color separations by iocolor, Seattle
Produced by Marquand Books, Inc., Seattle
    www.marquand.com
Printed and bound by C&C Offset Printing Co., Ltd., China

Photo credits:

All building photographs © Lara Swimmer except: pp. 9 and 11 by John W. Hubbard.

All photographs of artworks by Richard Nicol except: p. 29, Larry Bemm: photo by Dirk Park; p. 29, Paul Berger: courtesy of the artist; p. 31, David Darraugh: photo by Patrick Cusick; p. 32, Sally Finch: photo by Bill Bachhuber; p. 34, Fay Jones: photo by Eduardo Calderón; p. 35, Keith Lewis: photo by Doug Yaple; p. 36, Nancy Mee: photo by Spike Mafford; p. 37, Jeffry Mitchell: photo by Kate Elliott; p. 38, Barbara Noah: photo courtesy of the artist; p. 42, Kiff Slemmons: photo by Rod Slemmons; p. 45, Nancy Worden: photo by Lynn Hamrick.

Back cover and page 1: Steel engraving of three scenes of Mount Rainier by George Elbert Burr (United States, 1859–1939) published in John Muir, "Washington and the Puget Sound," from the series *Picturesque California, Oregon, Washington, Alaska, Idaho, Montana, Wyoming, Colorado, Utah, Nevada, Arizona, New Mexico; The Rocky Mountains and the Pacific Slope* part XVII (New York and San Francisco: J. Dewing Publishing Company, 1888): 282. Photo courtesy of MSCUA, University of Washington Libraries (neg. no. UW 22311).

CONTENTS

DIRECTOR'S FOREWORD **JANEANNE A. UPP**
6

ANTOINE PREDOCK'S TACOMA ART MUSEUM **PATRICIA MCDONNELL**
9

EDGEWISE IN NATURE **IVAN DOIG**
13

PRIDE OF PLACE IN THE NORTHWEST: BUILDING TRADITION **ROCK HUSHKA**
17

WORKS IN THE EXHIBITION
29

TACOMA ART MUSEUM STAFF
46

TACOMA ART MUSEUM BOARD OF TRUSTEES AND CAPITAL CAMPAIGN STEERING COMMITTEE
47

TACOMA ART MUSEUM MAJOR CONTRIBUTORS TO THE NEW BUILDING
48

New beginnings are always filled with dew-eyed promise. This is true even when it is actually a reincarnation and not a birth. In 2003, as a sixty-eight-year-old organization, Tacoma Art Museum starts a bright new future as we open the doors to a new state-of-the-art facility designed by renowned architect Antoine Predock.

Any organization, art museums included, flourishes because of the tenacity, imagination, heart, and hard work of the people engaged in it. Tacoma Art Museum has always had the great fortune to attract extraordinary supporters—be they staff, trustees, patrons, members, artists, or community museum-goers. Especially over the many years of planning and raising funds for the new facility, the generous spirit of the Tacoma and Puget Sound community has shone through at this regional art museum. More than 1,500 individuals, businesses, and foundations made the new building a reality through their contributions.

As a regional museum, Tacoma Art Museum takes seriously its role in the community. That conviction inspires the museum to seek out and celebrate the visual artists who are our neighbors. Presenting the creativity and rich subjects of artists who live in the Northwest has been a commitment of this museum since its inception. This commitment is realized anew in our 1701 Pacific Avenue building that has been carefully designed for the viewing of art and as a measure of place in this mist-filled, moss-laden region. Called a "deftly folded work of origami," the new building helps us to redouble the importance of Northwest art to the museum's mission.

Both these beliefs meet in the project *Building Tradition: Gifts in Honor of the Northwest Art Collection*. People of various walks of life generously gave works by Northwest artists. The additional 200 works are a boost to our distinguished, growing collection. And the sign of faith from museum supporters makes clear that, with such demonstrated loyalty, the Tacoma Art Museum's future can only sparkle—even on the most rain-soaked days.

JANEANNE A. UPP

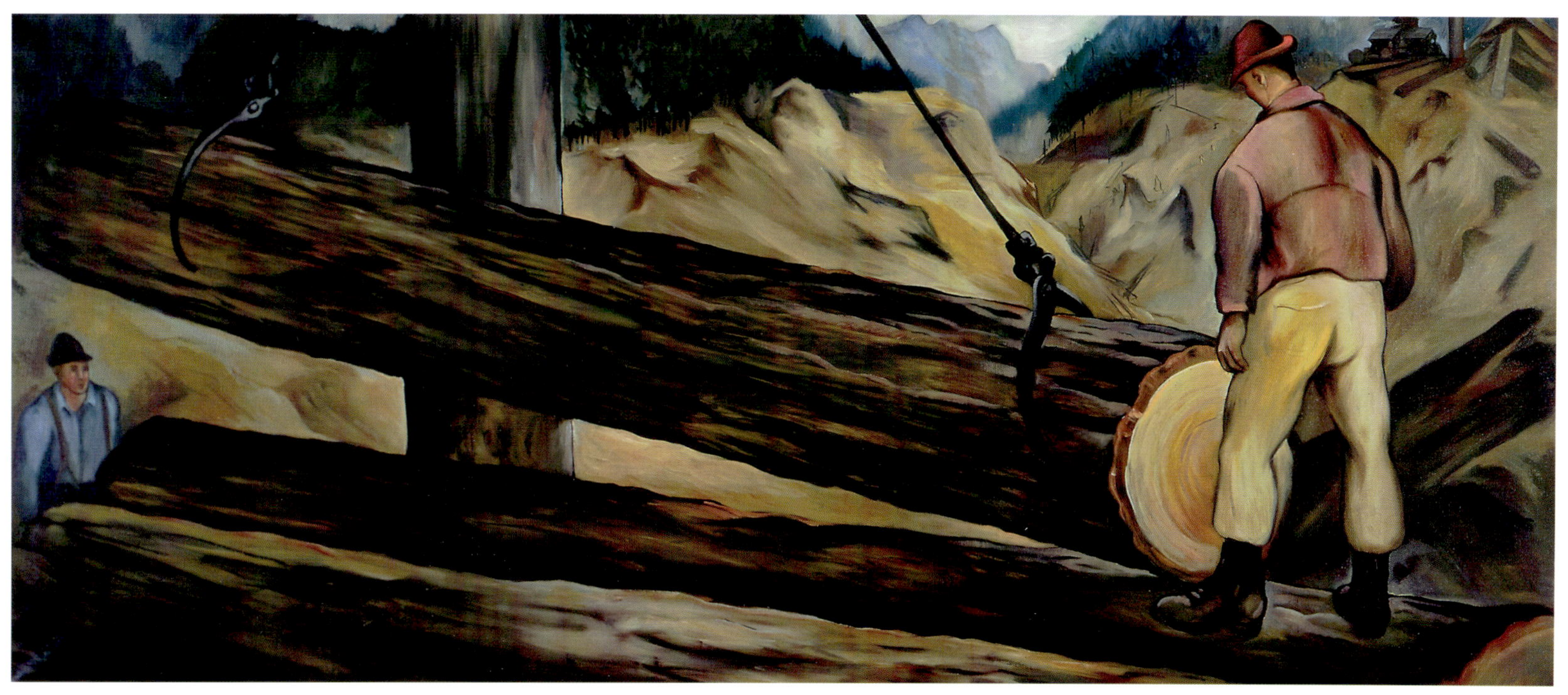

Kenneth Callahan
United States, 1905–1986
*Weyerhaeuser Company Mill B
mural panel*, 1944
Oil on canvas
48 × 105½ in.
Tacoma Art Museum, Gift of the
Weyerhaeuser Company

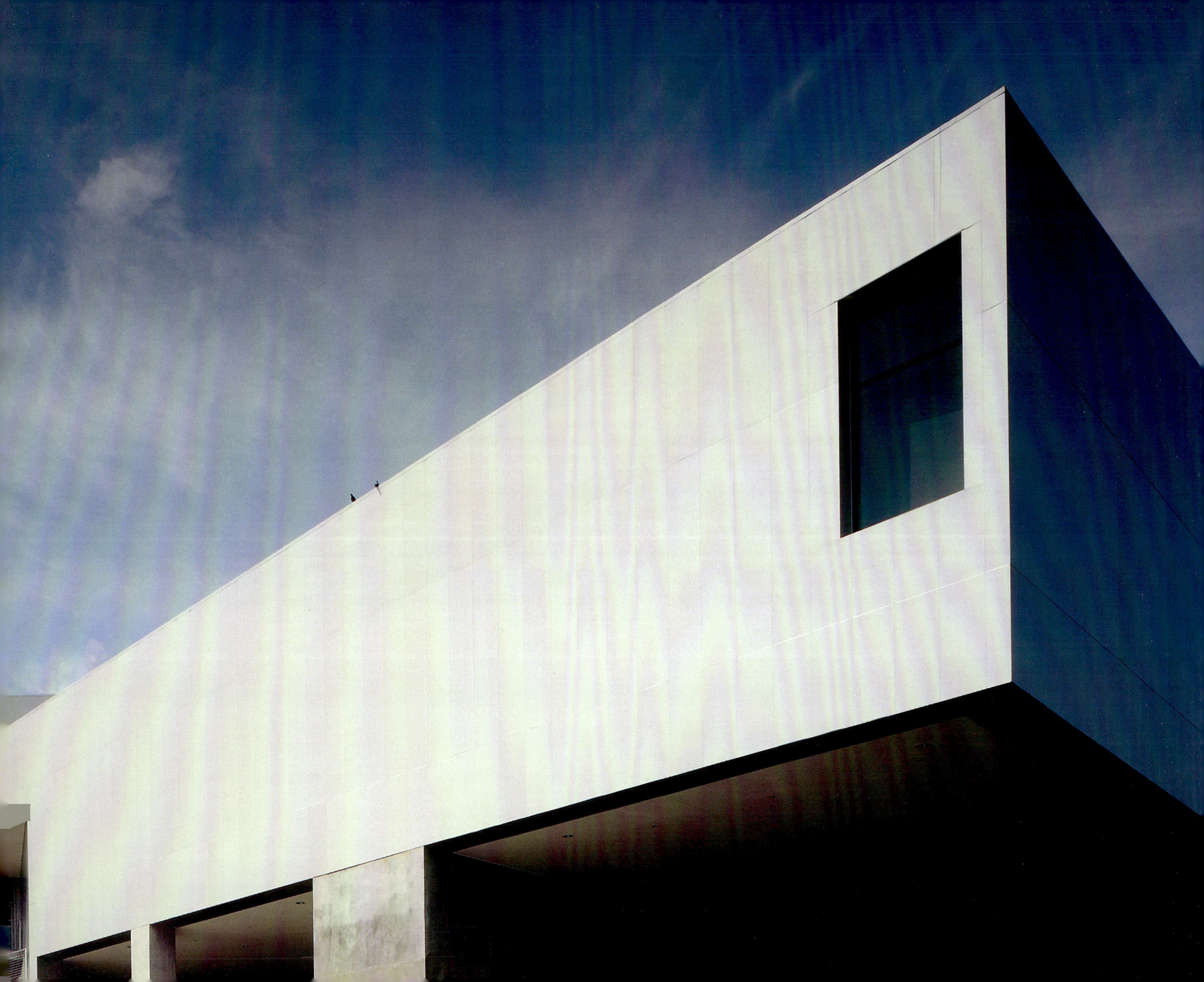

PATRICIA MCDONNELL

Architect Antoine Predock designed a 50,000-square-foot facility that meets the challenge of Tacoma Art Museum's mission as a regional museum deeply rooted in its community—to connect people through art. According to many art and architecture critics, he excelled at the task because the building functions wonderfully *and* is innovative and beautifully elegant—with "the form and lightness of a deftly folded work of origami."[1]

Understanding what it is like to live in a certain place or region, and reflecting that in his buildings, have been keys to Antoine Predock's success as an architect. As a result, his work does not fit comfortably into a stylistic niche. In Tacoma, the New Mexico–based Predock displayed great insight into the Pacific Northwest. The subtle transformations of Puget Sound's mist and oyster light clearly impressed the architect, as did the imposing Mount Rainier. Light and its ever-changing qualities accentuate the building's geometries with patterns of shadow and light that echo basic structural elements and with the light-filled stone garden as a centerpiece for the galleries. The looming Mount Rainier, an awe-inspiring landmark in Tacoma's Pierce County, is present in multiple and complex ways in the building, from the ascending ramp winding upward through the galleries, to the glistening stainless steel evoking icy heights, and the massing of forms that recall geologic rock formations. The steel surface, tall concrete columns, and concrete base recall the industrial past and reference the present for the busy port of Tacoma. In a statement that could serve as his architectural credo, Predock wrote: "We remind ourselves that we are involved in a timeless encounter with another place, not just a little piece of land. All of the readings that have accumulated there and been assimilated there, that are imagined there, that may happen there in the future—all of these collapse in time and become the raw material with which we interact."[2]

With signature evocations of the Northwest, the new Tacoma Art Museum building has also been rigorously designed for the viewing of art. On the exterior, the stainless steel skin of the low-slung building recedes in deference to surrounding historic structures. Inside, the building is an "ode to light," to quote another critic.[3] Twelve thousand square feet of galleries nestle around the central open-air stone garden. Designed by Seattle-based artist and landscape architect Richard Rhodes, the form of the garden sculpture is a silent wave, with undulating curves and textured stone that appear to dissolve into the sky in the atrium's reflective glass and steel. Natural light from the stone garden washes over the surrounding tall gallery walls, bringing the warmth of ambient light to viewing rooms while protecting the art from the harmful sun. Gallery rooms range from intimate to immense, and achieve the perfect curatorial balance—they have both rich architectural character and sufficient neutrality so artworks on exhibit claim museum-goers' first attention.

Inside wonderfully connects with outside at Tacoma Art Museum. Windows in the galleries provide surprising glimpses at the building's surroundings while the museum's magnificent entry offers a sweeping vista onto neighboring historic structures,

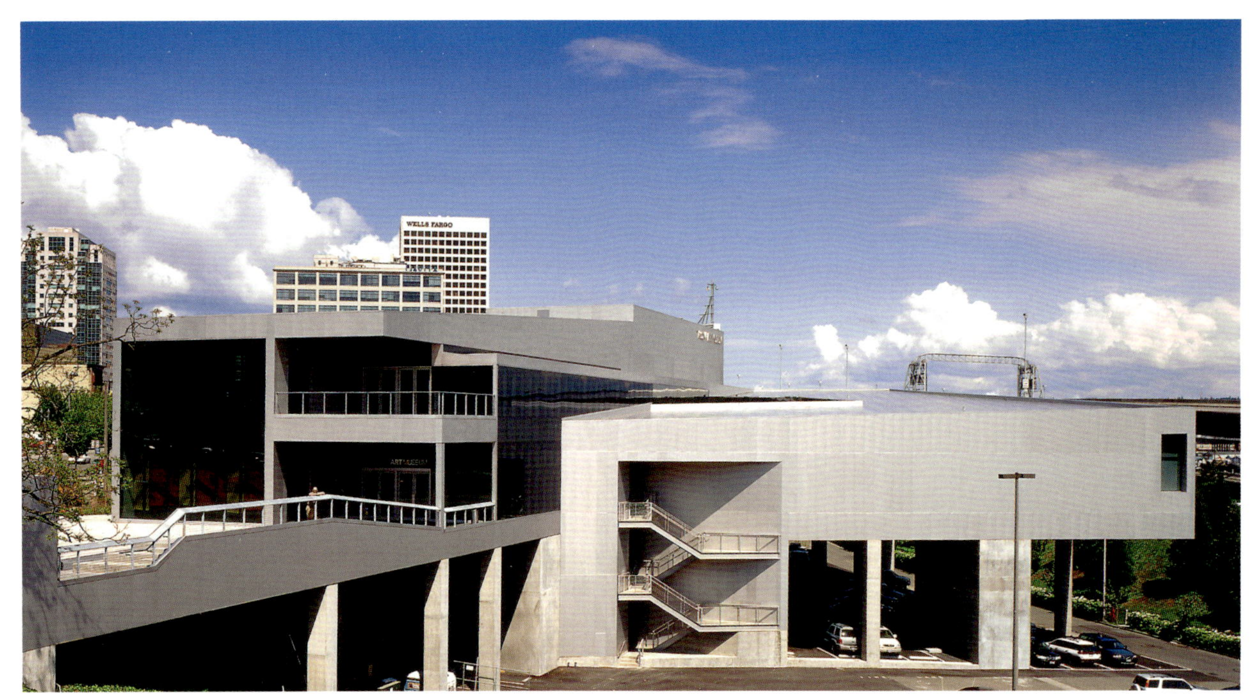

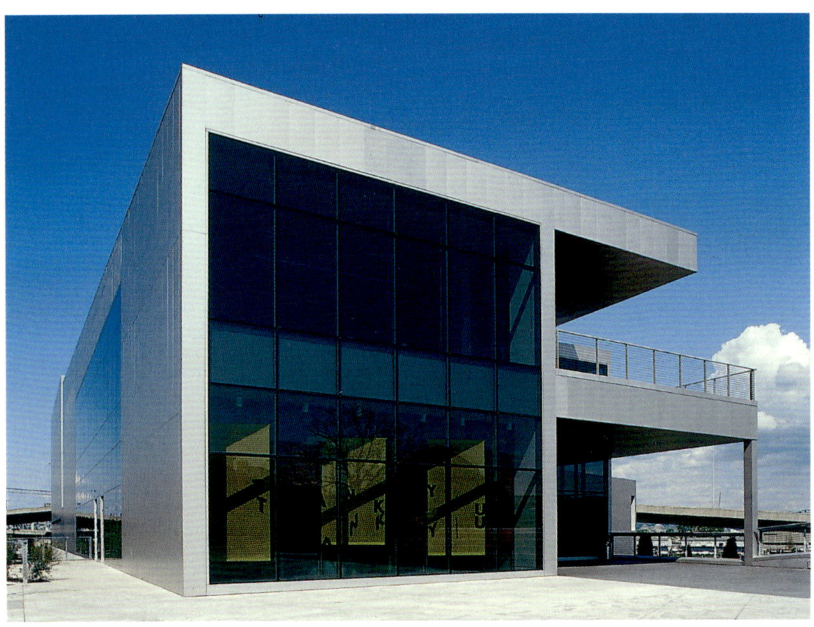

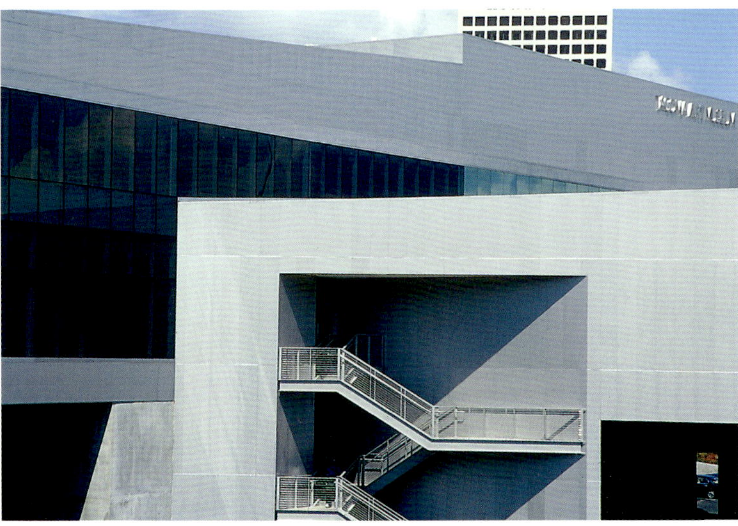

the port, and Mount Rainier. Views from the museum's education wing—where drop-in artmaking and library art research are always open to all—may be the most spectacular. Connecting sights of changing light, of interior and exterior views, and of artworks on display turn museum visitors to a special appreciation of visual experience—in a building and institution devoted to lifelong *visual* learning.

Although the 1701 Pacific Avenue museum is Predock's first structure in the Northwest, he is a leading figure in architecture nationally. Among his signature works are the Nelson Fine Arts Center at Arizona State University in Tempe, the Arizona Science Center in Phoenix, the Las Vegas Central Library and Discovery Museum, and the recently opened San Diego Padres stadium. He has been profiled in *Vanity Fair,* Rizzoli has published three books about his work, and he has received numerous national and international awards.

As noted architecture critic David Dillon said of Antoine Predock, "while his architecture remains consistently spare, planar, and primal, it is richly inflected by ideas and images."[4] This is certainly true for Tacoma Art Museum. The new building serves the museum extraordinarily well, and it raises the bar on how deftly architecture can enhance and foster the pleasure of viewing works of art.

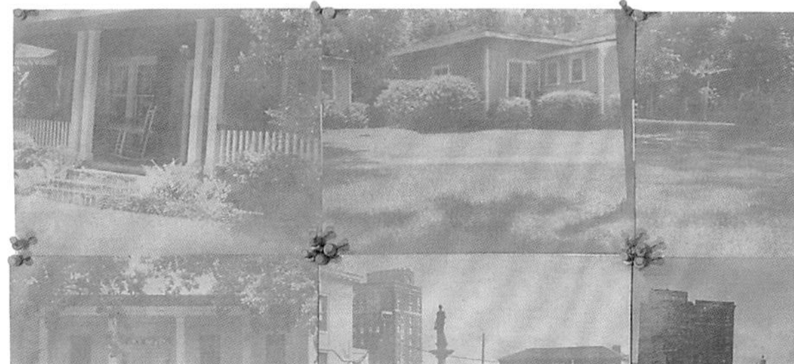

Patricia McDonnell is Chief Curator at Tacoma Art Museum.

Notes

1. Randy Gragg, "The Daredevil Architect and His Self-effacing Museum," *The Oregonian* (January 26, 2003): E2.

2. Antoine Predock, "Notes," *Antoine Predock Architect* (New York: Rizzoli, 1994), 14.

3. Sheila Farr, "Ode to Light," *Seattle Times* (April 27, 2003): K1, K3.

4. David Dillon, "Antoine Predock, American Visionary," *Architecture* (March 1995): 56.

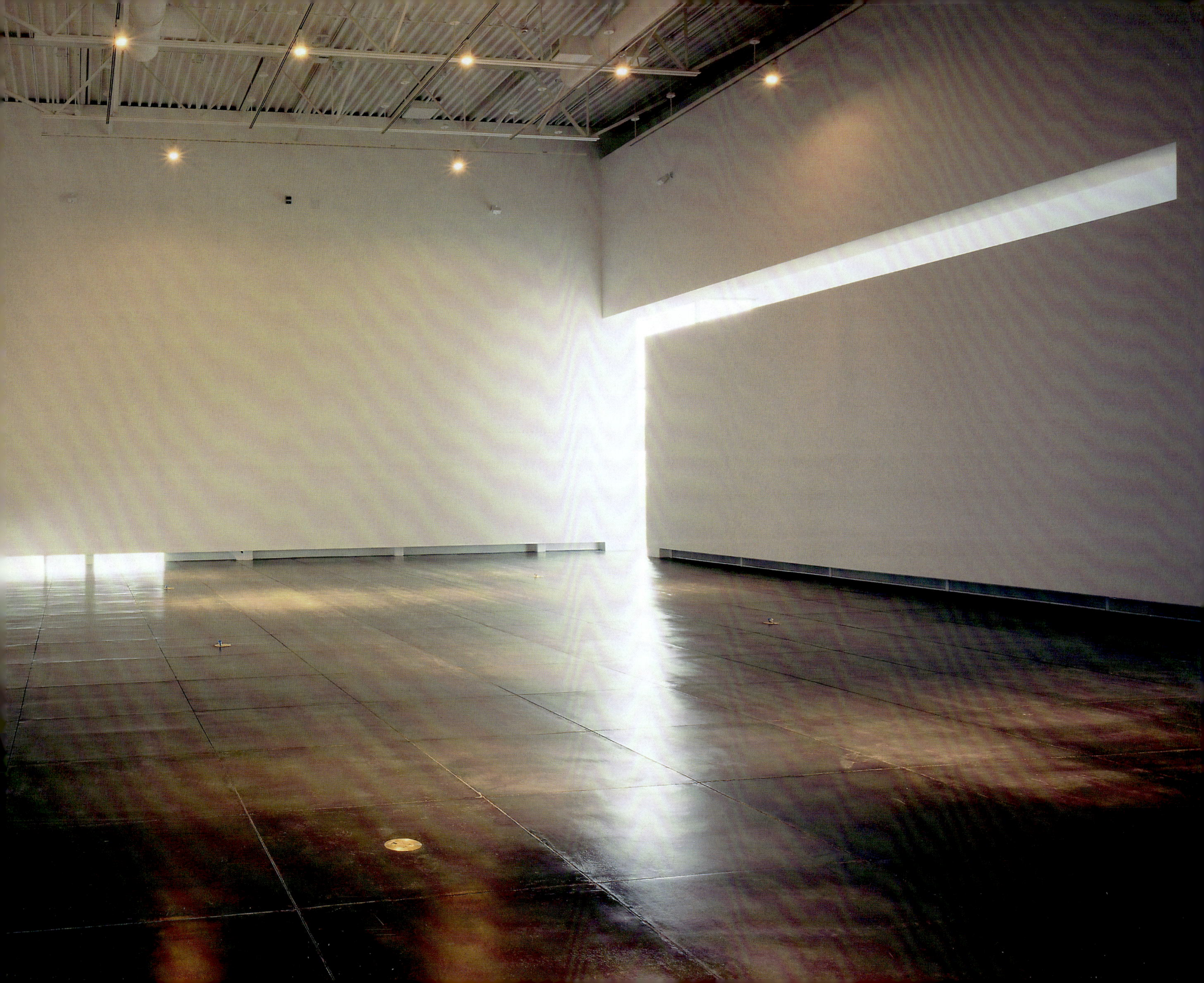

EDGEWISE IN NATURE

IVAN DOIG

The glass path of the water cuts south past the Puget Sound bluff where I write—the same nature-abounding height where artist Morris Graves once dreamt light onto canvas. This place, with its quintessential Northwest experience of height and edge, conclusively shapes my view of the world.

If you have followed the geography of discovery to Tacoma's spectacularly fresh new museum, you, too, share this view of the world. Here, the necessary edges of nature and art are conjoined in architecture and a tradition-building exhibition that promises so much exploration to come. Promontories, after all, are for getting out on the brink—continental or cultural—and looking around. Given the occasion and all the auspices that brought architect Antoine Predock's cloud-toned ark of art to rest on this outlook of city and mountain, let us consider the curiously beneficial breakage of landform and mind-set in the Northwest. Simply and grandly, the shaping edges of nature and the nature of edges influence both our everyday lives and our art.

By now, the Pacific Northwest has won the media's "livability" trophy enough times to retire it. But the rest of the nation's foggy view of us as shore-sitting coffee-swillers, located somewhere up-coast from La-La-Land and a trifle south of *Northern Exposure* reruns, misses the actuality of how deeply our surroundings touch into us.

We are something like remnant druids, those of us who choose to dwell out here. We dabble in the Puget Sound palette of light and water and keep daily company with old loved peaks. All the while fully knowing that this west-most break-off of the continent is reflective of the profound restlessness of the earth: the earthquake faults and volcanic forces that underlie this alluringly rumpled region. Mental paint-by-the-number landscapists, are we? Amateur fire-walkers just waiting for the lava? No, our dominant awareness of nature, so fundamentally a part of our minute-by-minute lives, is not simply visual pleasure nor an exhilaration about the outdoors enhanced by a sufficient bit of risk. Rather, it is an attunement to the flow of things—call it "geomemory"—that goes back far beyond us, a memory that we carry as a regional characteristic as distinctive as our rain hoods.

Geomemory, let us say, may be something like the phenomenon noted by the perceptive writer John McNulty when, for the first time he visited his ancestors' Ireland and experienced the feeling of going "back where I had never been." Nature takes that half-familiarity, half-strangeness and enwraps us in it tantalizingly wherever we point our boots. Different from our human sort, of course, it is the universe's sort—the cells of memory ticking away in tree rings, geological strata, the beaks of finches, and glaciated valleys—that we somehow overhear, faintly but compellingly and must puzzle out afresh, each time. Nature, the rememberer, imitates art in finding ways to tell its story over and over but never quite the same twice.

I speak here as a licensed practitioner of memory; written pages, after all, are a form of word-memory that we call "literature." As a writer interested in the lives of people on the verges of challenge-filled landforms—the Continental Divide of my native Rockies, and the green jigsawed

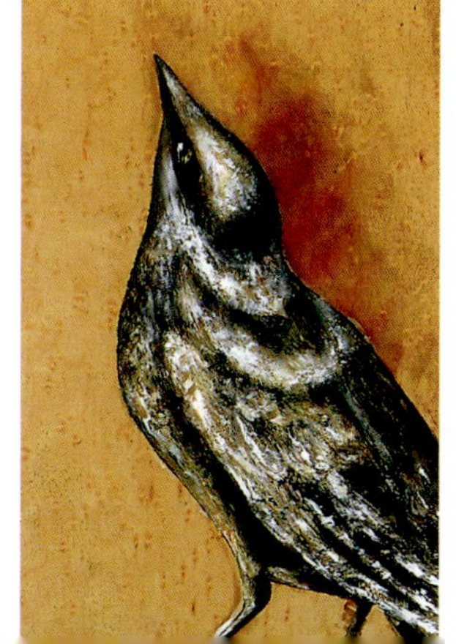

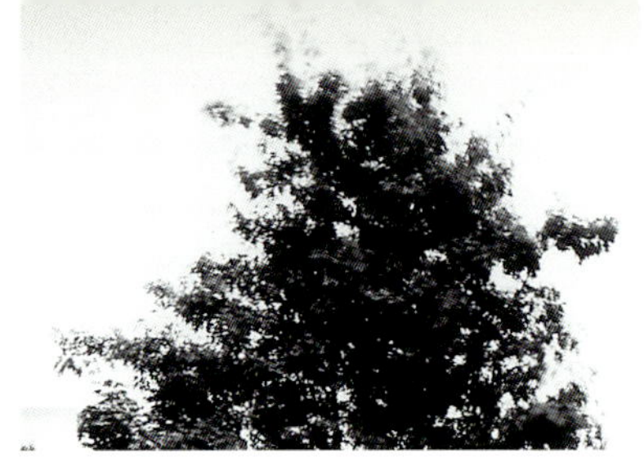

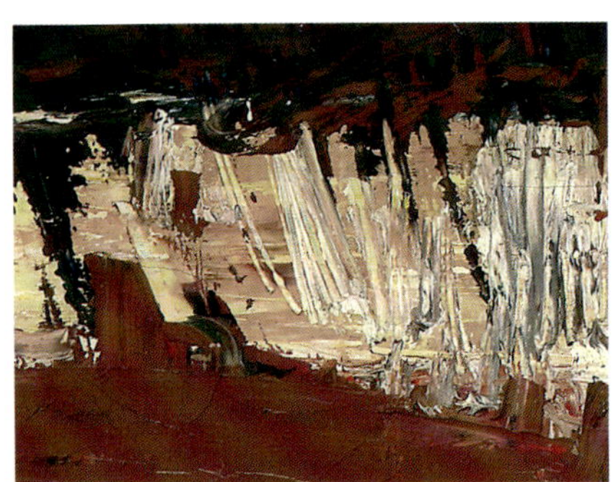

coastline that has lured and held me here—many of my pages happen to deal with what might be termed "world-memory." In short, the Earth's own memory, the topographical testimony of the planet's processes. Much of my daily work is to try to catch into print, in descriptive phrases and telling metaphors, nature's signature expressions. To seek the kinship between words and worlds, of course, is to peer forever over the edges of both, to see what can be brought from the depths of existence.

(By the way, such bits of linguistic delving are not confined to card-carrying writers. Everyone out here does it. If there is so much as a candleworth of sunlight, right now, stroll to a window facing the midsection of the Cascade mountain range. There it is: that geo-vulcanian totemic colossus—"the mountain." Mount Rainier, sky-sitting, candescent in its year-round light cloak of snow and ice. "Ah, ooh, oh," we say, "the mountain is out." Right there, the tongue dances a deft little step in deference to the dimension of nature. Notice how "the" puts a shaping edge to this image ever there somewhere on our horizon: our emblematic peak is singled out by that habitual little definite article, as if framing it in for full and proper appreciation.)

That, then, I believe is one of the brain seams where the edges of nature meet our own. By way of art, we evolve equally deep influences from the nature of edges—from the daring specificities of creativity, the brinks and breakthroughs where artists must venture for us.

That each individual artist necessarily maps this edge-hugging route to art does not always register with observers from afar when they glance toward our misty western shore. Time and again, I am asked by interviewers from the mysterious East (Coast) if there is a Northwest school of writing. Assuredly not, I tell them—minnows travel in schools. That answer is given at least as strongly by the historic work of artists out here whose one tradition in common is leviathan ideas:

- The fearlessly intricate coastal carvers of longhouse art, refusing to be circumscribed, as the immortal Haida artist Bill Reid put it, "by the silly feeling that it is impossible for two figures to occupy the same space at the same time."

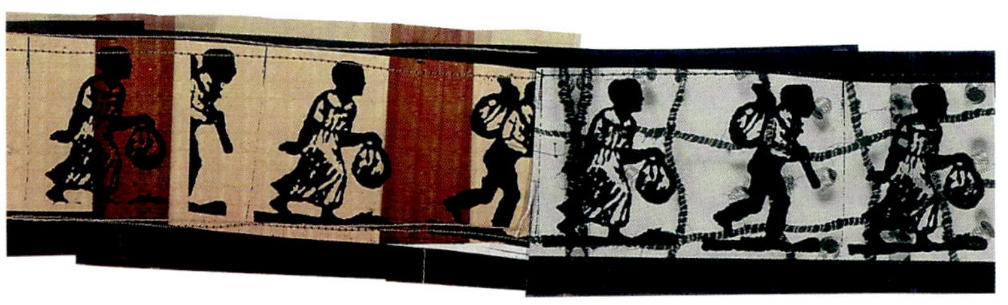

- The passages to Asia, and the magicianly excursions to capture light with the tip of a brush, achieved by that quartet of originals who happened to share Puget Sound as an address: Guy Anderson, Kenneth Callahan, Morris Graves, and Mark Tobey.

- The hot taproot to vulcanism that Dale Chihuly (and other artists) so successfully found in molten glass.

- And depend on it—some green young artist wandering these same shores, just now beginning to explore the peripheries of creation, will one day show us some startling new slant into our part of the world.

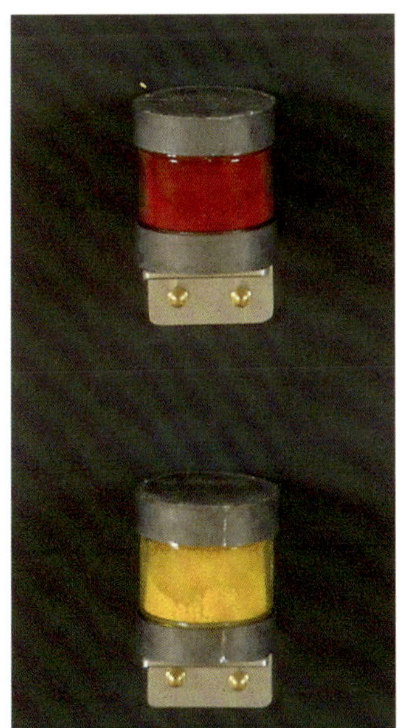

Does it actually matter, though, where on the map a maker of art happens to work? You bet it does. Locale is the whetstone on which talent sharpens itself. I see this all the time in my own field, the art of fiction, where a kind of locally rooted chance-taking has brought forth what I can only call the eloquence-of-the-edge-of-the-world. From the outback of Australia, the ethnic back pockets of India, the borderlands north of us in Canada, marvelously imaginative novels have been produced by writer after writer whose work, at first glance, seems to be far away from the self-appointed literary capitals of New York, London, and Paris. In fact, these word artists—edge-walkers all—have moved the central power of fiction to where they are in the world.

The art critic Kenneth Clark once traced this same pedigree of nervy drawing-on-your-own-roots in artists of other stripes as well. Clark was himself as inbred, upper-crust, snobby a Londoner as ever existed. Yet, at the end of a centuries-spanning examination of great works of art, his provocative conclusion (summarized by Bernard Bailyn, one of America's ablest historians of ideas) also points outward: "Artists on the periphery introduce simplicity and common sense to a style that has become too embellished, too sophisticated, too self-centered. . . . And they have a visionary intensity, which at times attains a lyrical quality, as they celebrate the world around them and strive to realize their fresh ambitions."[1]

The necessity of fresh ambitions. Kenneth Clark and I, from the vantage points of our respective fields, probably do not have a single thing in common other than that shared belief. Of how vital it is for a people, a region, a society, to have art always making its way into our lives from new and unexpected directions.

Artists out here need to be edgewise in nature, so to speak, in more ways than one: conversant with risk and comfortable wrapped in this gray-green coast. One of my novelist compatriots, Australian-born Shirley Hazzard, once said that the articulation we know as art springs from the oldest, deepest, most memorious longing: to relieve the soul of incoherence. We, too, edge up on that soul relief when we contemplate what is housed and will be housed in this gravity-breaking art museum.

Seattle-resident Ivan Doig is the author of seven novels and three works of nonfiction, including the just-published *Prairie Nocturne*. His writing has won high praise for its attentiveness to the Western experience and masterful prose style. He is a National Book Award finalist and the winner of the Western Literature Association's Distinguished Achievement Award.

Note

1. Bernard Bailyn, *To Begin the World Anew* (New York: Alfred A. Knopf, 2003), 7, quoting Kenneth Clark, *Moments of Vision* (New York: Harper & Row, 1981), 50–62.

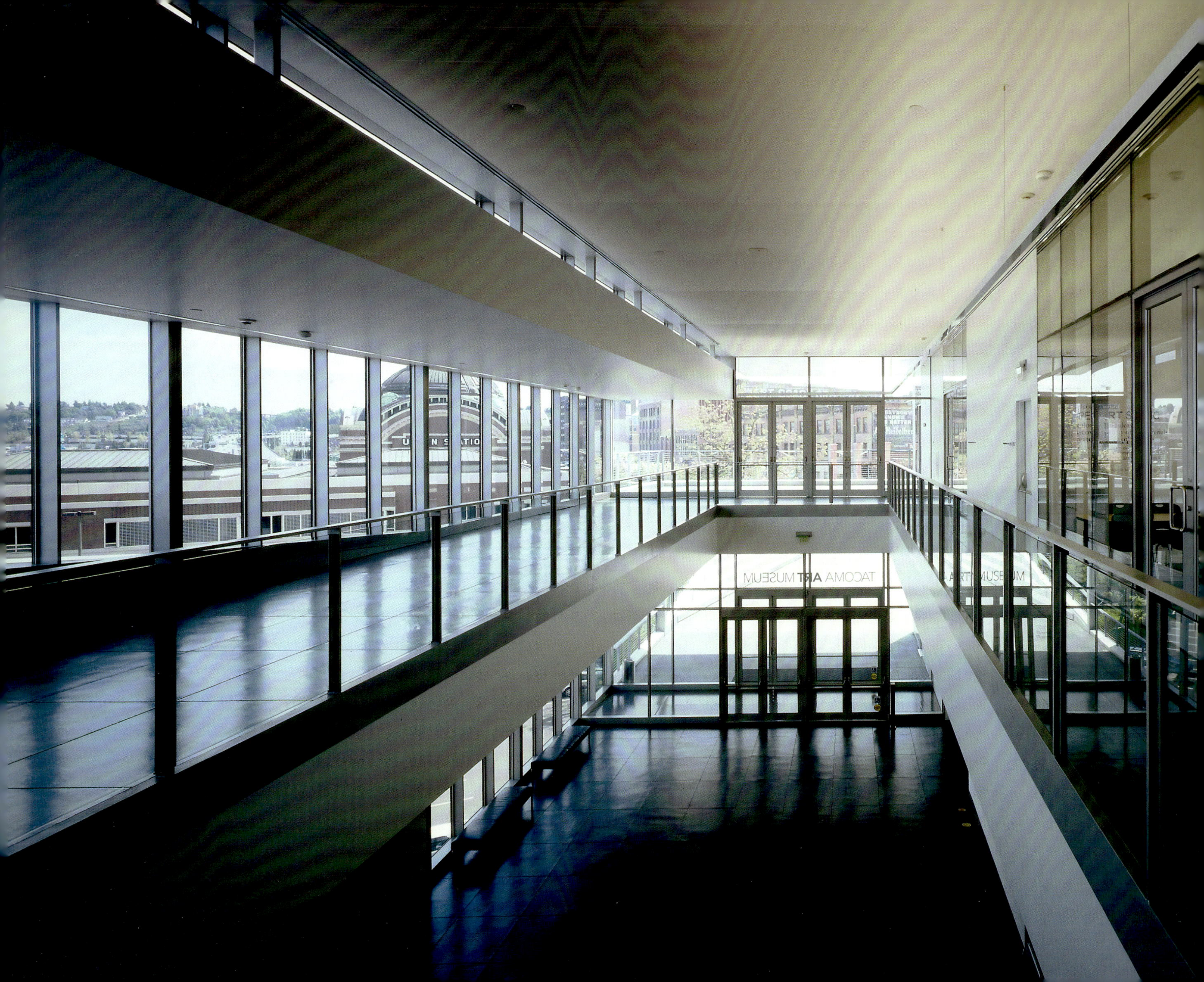

ROCK HUSHKA

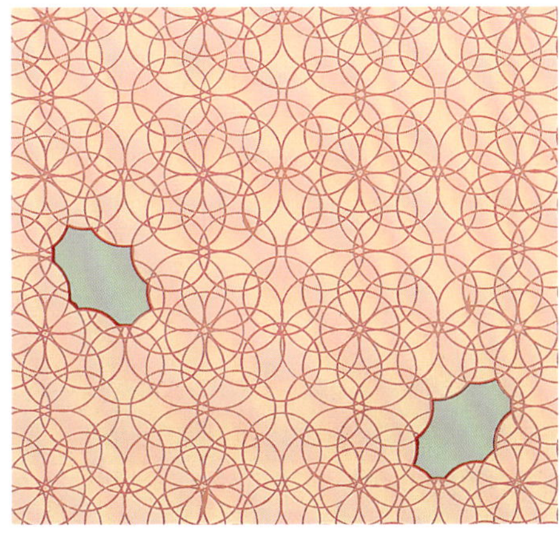

For those who live in the Northwest, a handful of truly monumental things—from nature, from commerce, from culture—dominate our self-perception: Mount Rainier and Mount Hood, the Columbia River and Puget Sound, Microsoft and Nike, the legacies of Kurt Cobain and Jimmy Hendrix, Matt Groening, Oregon's high desert, the Hoh Rain Forest in the Olympic National Park, and enormous individual fortunes amassed during the boom years of recent decades. The sense of achievement and local pride instilled by these regional icons rest uneasily next to the unmistakable dominance of distant influences such as California's trends and the major East Coast cultural institutions.

The perpetual mix of inside and outside influences is particularly challenging for the region's artists. Hard-earned achievements in local galleries and regional museums are difficult to duplicate elsewhere. Artists often must decide between maintaining their involvement with their community or seeking greater fortunes in international artistic centers such as London, New York, or Los Angeles. Additionally, local gallery owners, collectors, and curators seek to promote the work and vision of the region's artists while also understanding how local art relates to national and, increasingly, international trends. In essence, meaningful advocacy for Northwest art becomes a complicated quest for development, balance, and rigor.

Since its inception as the Tacoma Art Association in 1935, Tacoma Art Museum (TAM) has embraced the art and artists of the Pacific Northwest while also bringing extraordinary art of an international caliber to the region. Through its exhibitions and programs, TAM has offered exceptional opportunities to experience exhibitions featuring paintings by Vincent van Gogh, the quilts of Faith Ringgold, Soviet conceptual art, ceramics of Pablo Picasso, video by Bill Viola, and the photographs of Gordon Parks, among many others.

The variety of artistic impulses that shaped the exhibition programming also guided the development of the museum's permanent collection. The task of assembling a permanent collection began only when the Tacoma Art League (the former Tacoma Art Association) officially incorporated as the Tacoma Art Museum in 1963. Strategically, the initial acquisitions were paintings by notable Northwest artists. In forty years as a collecting institution, TAM has acquired 2,900 objects, of which approximately sixty percent are works by Northwest artists.

TAM's exhibition history, permanent collection, and educational programming reflect the pride of place given to the region's art. In February 2001, the museum's board of trustees refined TAM's mission and vision statement reaffirming the institution's commitment to Northwest art: "TAM serves the diverse communities of the Northwest through its collection, exhibitions, and learning programs, emphasizing art and artists from the Northwest."

Building Tradition: Gifts in Honor of the Northwest Art Collection acknowledges TAM's steadfast commitment to the region's artists while celebrating the most auspicious moment in the institution's history—the opening of the elegant, new museum building at 1701 Pacific Avenue. This exhibition

When morning is come above the Cascades, the air of the valleys rises
before it [Mount Rainier] in a faint, silver mist like some exhalation of
the dawn. It becomes invisible sometimes for hours and, when slowly
it reappears, it seems to have been transformed into another mountain.
Its foreground of forest is turned to greener blue. Its lines are etched
rather than chiseled. One sees the blue of its crags and rock-falls, its
mottlings of shadowed snow, and the glisten of its upper icefields. As
the sun westerns, it grows even more aloof from the world of men. Some
days it looks like a vast, dim snowdrift swept up out of the hinterland;
on other days, it is all a wild gleam and indistinguishable surge of mountain and cloud; again it seems disparted from the earth altogether and
soars to an incredible height, a very phantom of the air, shadowless,
colorless, almost formless. And then comes sunset, which is the hour
of its transfiguration. A faint purple steals over the water, and the
forests darken into velvet.

Robert Walkinshaw, 1929

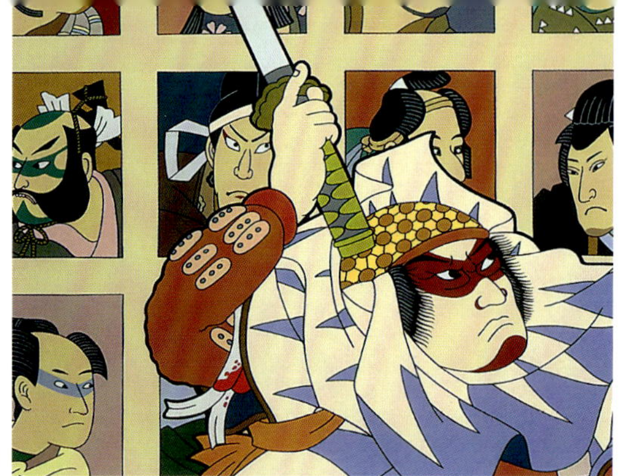

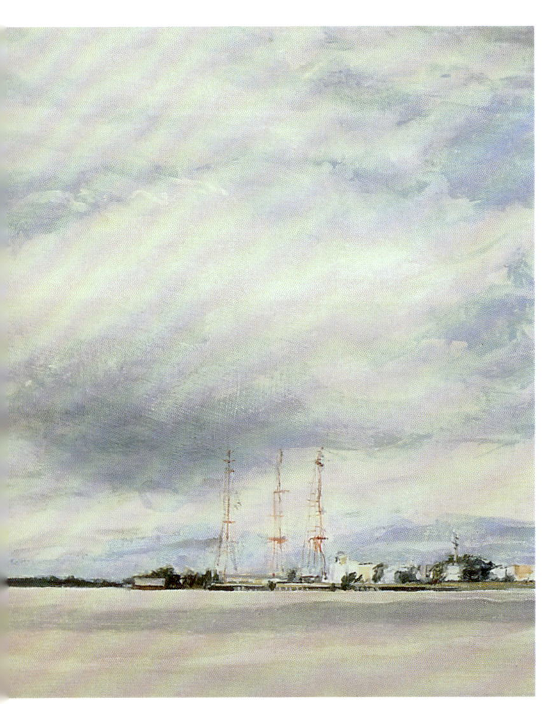

series and catalogue continue TAM's venerable
tradition of marking each new phase of the institution's history with an important exhibition of
Northwest art. Through the generosity of artists,
collectors, gallery owners, and TAM trustees, more
than 200 new works have been added to the museum's permanent collection.

The acquisitions of *Building Tradition* provide a
snapshot of the history and potential of Northwest
art. The project's primary goals were to strengthen
TAM's permanent collection and to reaffirm TAM's
commitment to the artists of the region. The orga-
nizing principle was to create a project suggesting
the concept of the *Kunstkammer,* a collection of
beauteous wonders.[1]

The art that constitutes the *Building Tradition* project reflects the broad diversity of artistic
activity in the Northwest and stands as testament
to the inexhaustible creative forces at play in the
region. Some works are classically beautiful, and
others possess a more esoteric aesthetic that urges
deeper contemplation. Traditional works such as
landscape images mix with unexpected objects such
as abstract sculptures of miniscule scale. The works
range in media from egg tempera painting to digital video to bullet holes. The artists live and work
across the Northwest—most live in the Seattle
and Portland metro areas; some thrive in eastern
Washington, Montana, and Idaho; and some have
left for opportunities outside the region. Perhaps
most importantly, this exhibition offers a glimpse
of the intellectual, aesthetic, and emotional power
of the artists working in the Northwest since the
early 1930s.

Northwest Fantasy by Mark Tobey, *Minidoka
No. 5 (442nd)* by Roger Shimomura, and *Choker
#83* by Mary Lee Hu have distinguished exhibition
histories. Some works, most notably the paintings
by Gaylen Hansen, Robert Helm, William Ivey,
Francesca Sundsten, and Robert Yoder, were given
because of the passions of distinguished collectors.

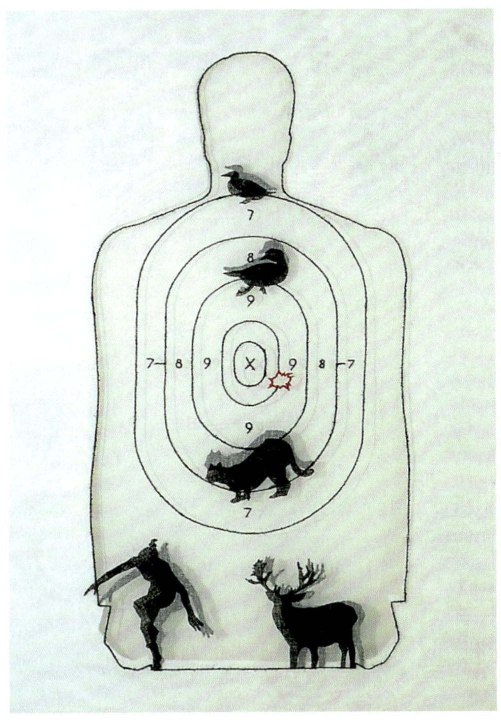

The works by Ellen George, Sally Finch, and Cynthia Toops represent an extraordinary engagement with strange and wonderful media. The works by Michael Ehle, Ron Ho, and Keith Lewis poignantly address the suffering and loss related to the AIDS crisis. Acquiring works by emerging artists was a crucial task (a partial list includes Eric Bashor, Patrick Holderfield, Kevin Kadar, Megan Murphy, Yuki Nakamura, Susan Seubert, Sarah Ellen Taylor, and Jennifer West). Victoria Adams, Phil Baldwin, Rachel Brumer, and Dennis Evans made objects specifically for this project that reflect their appreciation of TAM's engagement with local artists. Many artists were identified because they were not represented in the museum's collection — Sally Cleveland, David Darraugh, Laura Ross-Paul, Barbara Earl Thomas, and Terry Toedtemeier. Other artists, who have built national reputations such as David E. Chatt and Layne Goldsmith, are included because they remain underrepresented in the Northwest. Many of the artists have played important roles as mentors and teachers, such as Royal Nebeker, Ramona Solberg, Melissa Weinman, Christian Staub, among a host of others. Nancy Worden, Merrill Wagner, and Marita Dingus have special connections to the TAM family through their generous involvement in exhibitions and educational programs over the course of years.

This diverse group of artworks provides a timely opportunity to reconsider what is meant by the label "Northwest art." The notion of Northwest art as separate and distinct from any other sort of American art has bedeviled artists working in the region since the 1953 *Life* magazine article "Mystic Painters of the Northwest," which heralded the existence of a Northwest School to mainstream America.[2] Inevitably, a stereotype developed that the "Northwest artist" painted with a muted palette of various shades of muddy gray and harbored an abiding desire to paint images based on East Asian symbolism. Such artists were thought to be impervious to recent stylistic developments in the important art centers such as New York, and resistant to major developments including color field painting, pop, and minimal art.

Northwest artists struggled mightily against such stereotypes for decades, even as local and national critics repeatedly explained that such categorization did not apply. After seeing the exhibition of conceptual art, *557,087*, sponsored by the Seattle

White Mountain was a man. He had two wives and stood midway between them. The two women became angry with one another and started to fight. The one at the south threw fire at Mount Ranier [*sic*] (*taqoˊmən*). The fire hit Ranier but she threw it back at her rival. They kept this up. Finally, Ranier got struck very badly and her head broke off. The other woman got the best of her.

Tcihoˊł (James Cheholts, [Lower Cowlitz]), 1927

We had enjoyed, from the summit of a hill twenty miles south of Salem [Oregon], one of the most magnificent views in all earthly scenery. Within a single sweep of vision were seven snow peaks,—the Three Sisters, Mount Jefferson, Mount Hood, Mount Adams, and Mount St. Helens,—with the dim suggestion of an eighth colossal mass, which might be Rainier. All these rose along an arc of not quite half the horizon, measured between ten and eighteen thousand feet in height, were nearly conical, and absolutely covered with snow from base to pinnacle.

Fitz Hugh Ludlow, 1870

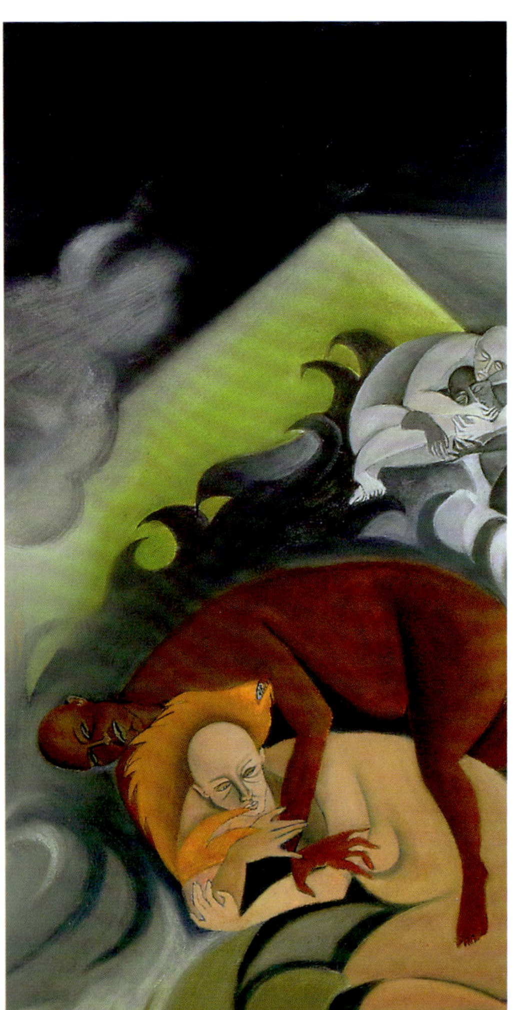

Art Museum in 1968, art critic Tom Robbins (who later wrote the quirky novels *Even Cowgirls Get the Blues* and *Half Asleep in Frog Pajamas*) penned a darkly humorous and cantankerous denunciation of the stereotype: "Let us hurry to seize the term 'Northwest Art,' nail it in a Haida coffin, weight it down with a ton of bronze bird sculptures and sink it in the deepest part of Puget Sound, marking the spot with a buoy decorated by quasi-Chinese calligraphers in order that innocent sailboats and carefree yellow submarines might keep their distance."[3] Robbins considered Northwest Coast formline designs, Asian symbolism, and Asian painting techniques as a mortal pox that afflicted the artists of the region. He insisted that good, strong art has no regional character but rather depends on the quality of intellectual content and the technical execution of the work. Virtually every ten years since *Life* outlined the existence of a Northwest School, an outside voice echoed Robbins's deductions that Northwest art was richly varied and of remarkable quality that matched the best art produced elsewhere.

Even so, critics continued to express surprise. After jurying an exhibition of eastern Washington painting in 1968, influential curator and art historian Peter Selz noted with a bit of surprise, "I was impressed by the high quality of some of the work . . . and the absence of any vestige of regionalism."[4] His comments introduced an article by Robbins that trumpeted the high standards and aspirations of artists working in the region.[5] In 1976, critic and curator Lucy Lippard somewhat imperiously conceded, "that there is plenty of energy, plenty of visual intelligence and plenty of up-to-date art knowledge in the Northwest. The real problem, here as in other places isolated from the art markets of the world, will be how to survive, how to maintain that energy, how to set up situations which nourish and focus it."[6]

The San Francisco–based critic, curator, and art historian Bill Berkson wrote a two-part report for *Art in America* in 1986 in which he explored the Seattle art scene. Cribbing from another remark by Robbins written in 1968 about the

Northwest's "curious spectrum of provincialism and hip," Berkson accurately observed that artists in the 1980s missed little of the "latest frissons worldwide but have determined to base themselves in the communities around Puget Sound" in their quest to enjoy the region's "civilized living conditions" and educational programs. The bulk of his first installment, more importantly, explored the various artist-run organizations and the flowering of public art programs in Seattle. For Berkson, the "alertness to new developments in major centers" and the high levels of artist activities in the region signaled a healthy arts community filled with opportunities.[7]

In his second installment he positively described nearly every possible type of art being created in Seattle: figurative and imagistic; abstract, realist, and otherwise; sculpture (noting the rise of ceramic and glass as serious media for serious artists); hybrids, tableaux, and computers; and photography. Commenting on the stereotype of a Northwest artist, Berkson observed, "It draws a blank from younger artists, many of whom come

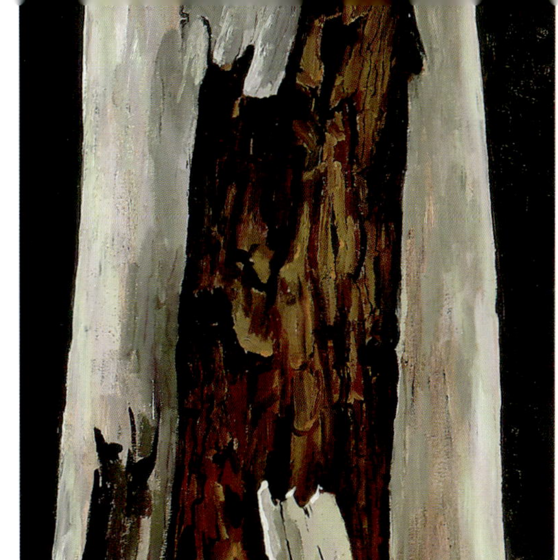

from elsewhere, relate to other traditions and, when told they do or don't fit a particular 'Northwest' mold, are suitably nonplussed."[8] Fleshing out his argument from the first installment, he emphasized that the region's pluralism sustained its vitality not an allegiance to an imaginary Northwest School.

Critics Berkson, Lippard, and Selz used their status as detached outsiders of the Northwest art world to conclude that regional efforts meshed with concurrent activities in New York. Their revelations highlight one of the core issues of provincialism: the complex interdependence between the metropolitan center and the outlying regions.

In 1974, the Australian critic Terry Smith presented a nuanced analysis of the provincialism conundrum.[9] Smith described the shifting power relationships (who is accepted, who decides what is new and noteworthy, what retains its value), the pitfalls of regional artists working at home, and the artists' role in perpetuating the status quo. He concluded that the ultimate responsibility for an artist's success depends squarely on his or her ability to generate an honest self-assessment in terms of individual development in both regional and metropolitan contexts. The region's arts specialists—art historians, collectors, critics, curators—must also accept this same responsibility to fulfill professional expectations as well as develop the self-confidence to look carefully and critically at the objects and ideas, which are generated locally. The wit and spunk that characterized Tom Robbins's writing in the late 1960s and early 1970s still resonate today as a reminder of the value of sustaining a critical discourse about the region's art.

Between 1983 and 1997, critic, freelance curator, and art historian Ron Glowen contributed a

The weather was serene and pleasant, and the country continued to exhibit, between us and the eastern snowy range, the same luxuriant appearance. At its northern extremity, mount Baker bore by compass N. 22 E.; the round snowy mountain, now forming its southern extremity, and which, after my friend Rear Admiral Rainier, I distinguished by the name of MOUNT RAINIER, bore N. [S.] 42 E.

Captain George Vancouver, 1792

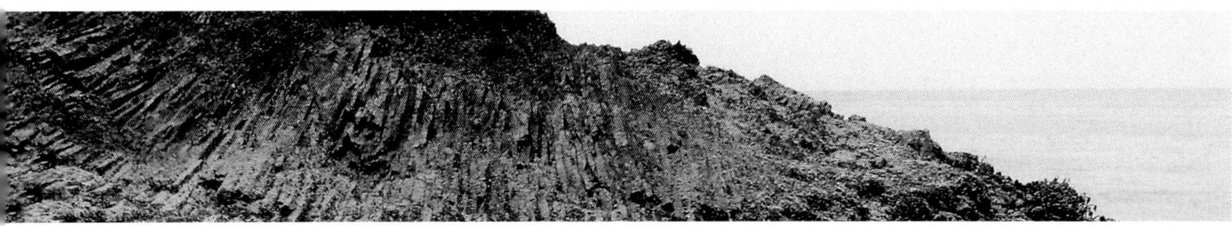

series of short essays to *Artweek* surveying the art in the Northwest with an emphasis on Seattle.[10] More cautious than Robbins, Glowen nonetheless explored the strengths of individual artists working in the region, while asking difficult questions about the long-term vitality of the Northwest artists' community. In 1991 Patricia Failing, critic and professor of art history at the University of Washington, compared and contrasted the art scenes of Seattle, Portland, and Vancouver, B.C. Her essay "The Pacific Northwest: Sex, Landscape, and Videotape" (a pun on the 1989 indie film *Sex, Lies, and Videotape*) detailed the emergence of gender politics, shifting patronage patterns, and a demand for cultural diversity. She found a region expanding its range of interests, its success in the marketplace, and its institutions.[11] Five years later, Regina Hackett, longtime art critic for the *Seattle Post-Intelligencer,* echoed Failing's sentiment and neatly summarized the broad range of art production in Seattle: "Within Seattle's exuberant arts scene, studio glass, defying all expectations of what glass should look like and what it can do when displayed in the home, has ushered in a freewheeling, can-do sensibility that permeates the other arts in this hilly, often foggy, frequently rained-on town. Painting and sculpture thrive here too, and so do crafts and the design arts."[12] Most recently, newly transplanted curators Lisa Corrin of the Seattle Art Museum and Elizabeth Brown of the University of Washington's Henry Art Gallery, submitted their early impressions in "The Mountain Is Out" for the British art magazine *Modern Painters.* Corrin and Brown placed their emphasis on the potential of Seattle's younger artists to participate in a global arena,

> The prevailing sense of possibility and evolving identity is so Seattle. The weather appears relentlessly grim, but then the fog lifts and one sees in every direction the

Directly in front, and apparently not over two miles distant, although really twenty, old Takhoma loomed up more gigantic than ever. We were far above the level of the lower snow-line on Takhoma. The high peak upon which we clung seemed the central core or focus of all the mountains around, and on every side we looked down vertically thousands of feet, deep down into vast, terrible defiles, black and fir-clothed, which stretched away until lost in the distance and smoke.

Hazard Stevens, 1876

We arrived at the Cloud Camp at noon, but no clouds were in sight, save a few gauze-ornamental wreathes adrift in the sunshine. Out of the forest at last there stood the mountain, wholly unveiled, awful in bulk and majesty, filling all the view like a separate, new-born world, yet withal so fine and so beautiful it might well fire the dullest observer to desperate enthusiasm. Long we gazed in silent admiration, buried in tall daisies and anemones by the side of a snowbank.

John Muir, 1888

endless volcanic peaks of the Olympics to the west, Cascades to the east, Mt. Baker to the north, and to the south, the imperious Mt. Rainier. When the Seattle art community says, 'the mountain is out,' it is staring at a cliché as well as the reality —the challenging peak it must scale to both stake its claim and get a panoramic view of what lies beyond the northwest [*sic*] region.[13]

They provided an abbreviated list of artists, who were tuned into the broader, stylistic currents of cutting-edge art. What is interesting is how often Northwest artists have scaled this metaphorical mountain.

Consider the case of Northwest photographers. In the 1890s, pioneering female photographers Myra Wiggins, Sarah Ladd, and Lily White gained national attention. Edward S. Curtis and Imogen Cunningham maintained studios in Seattle's Pioneer Square in the early twentieth century. In the 1920s, the Seattle Camera Club, a group of Japanese-American photographers (joined by a few white artists, among them Ella McBride) exhibited internationally until the internment of the Japanese-Americans by Executive Order 9066 in 1942. Bill Ritchie, to continue the example further, earned respect as a pioneer in video art in the early 1970s. By the mid-1980s, Ritchie and a handful of other artists, who still live and work in the Northwest including Paul Berger, Karen Guzak, and Nori Sato, were at the forefront of the digital art movement.

Likewise, Morris Graves and Mark Tobey swirled through the post–World War II zeitgeist and explored universal symbols and personal experience in parallel with the most "advanced" work on the national scene.[14] Contrary to the generally accepted stereotypes, Graves and Tobey worked through the lessons of symbolism, WPA-influenced figuration, cubism, and surrealism to create works of immense power and beauty.

These same patterns of artistic development can be found repeating in practically every medium—in glass, the art of Dale Chihuly and Ginny Ruffner; in ceramics, the art of Howard Kottler and Patti Warashina; in weaving, the art of Jack Lenor Larsen; in video, the art of Gary Hill; in performance, the projects of Dennis Evans; and in merging conceptual art with craft-based media, the art

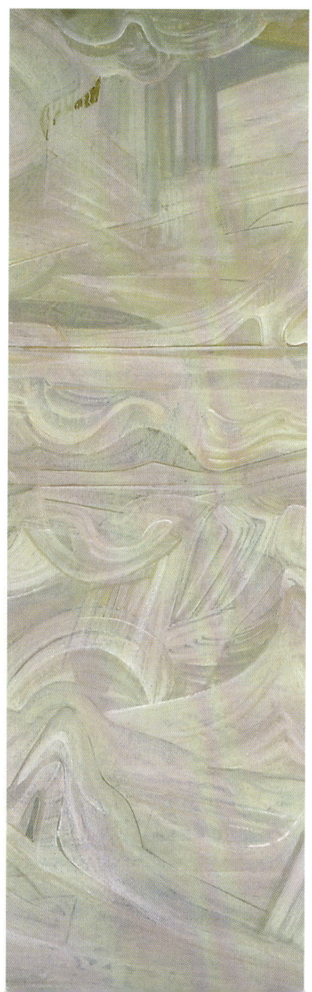

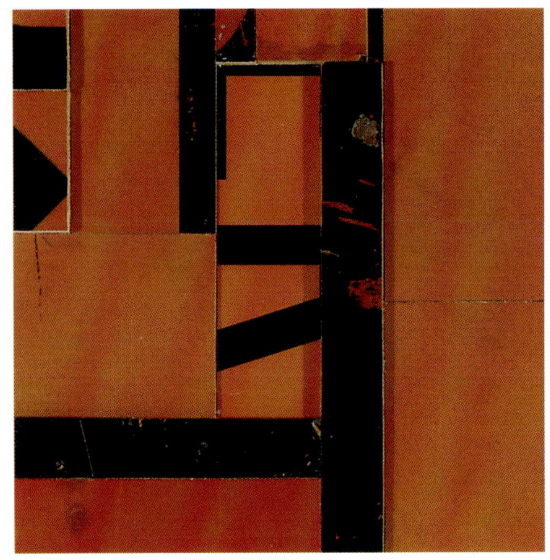

of Roy McMakin and Joshia McElheny. One simply needs to take the time to dust off the history by reviewing materials in the local libraries and by talking with artists, collectors, and gallery owners, and then shake off the self-negating impulses of provincialism. Yet, despite the undisputed national and international success of artists such as Chihuly and Cunningham—or paradoxically because of them—the artists of the Northwest remain held by the virtually unbreakable bonds of provincialism in the art world; as are the artists working in Atlanta, Denver, Houston, and Minneapolis. Perhaps the only way out of this bind is to follow Terry Smith's admonitions to think for ourselves and to maintain our own high expectations.

Consequently, it becomes one of the most important responsibilities of TAM, and similar museums, to preserve and promote the legacy of regional artists through strategic acquisitions as well as thoughtful and innovative exhibition and educational programming. TAM is fortunate in that, from its inception in 1935, Northwest art has been integral to the institution's goals. *Building Tradition* stands as testament to our institution's commitment to the art of the region. It signals a belief in the region's vitality and strengthens the museum's involvement with artists, collectors, and gallery owners, who live and work in our communities.

Building Tradition: Gifts in Honor of the Northwest Art Collection represents a sort of plateau in the metaphorical landscape dominated by monumental peaks like Mount Rainier and Mount Hood. It is an achievement for which the museum should be justly proud; but, TAM must continue to move upwards toward the summit.

Rock Hushka is Associate Curator at Tacoma Art Museum.

Notes

1. The concept *Kunstkammer* developed from the medieval treasuries of the aristocracy and religious orders. The word *Kunstkammer* first appeared in 1550 to describe the collection of paintings, precious objects, and natural science specimens amassed by the Holy Roman Emperor Ferdinand I (1503–1564, *reg* 1558–64). For a short history of the development of the *Kunstkammer,* see Elisabeth Scheicher, "Kunstkammer," in *The Dictionary of Art,* edited by Jane Tuerner, vol. 18 (London: Grove, 1996): 520–23.

2. Dorothy Seiberling, "Mystic Painters of the Northwest," *Life* vol. 35 (September 28, 1953): 84–89.

3. Tom Robbins, "Plague upon the Land," *Northwest Art News and Views* vol. 1 (January–February 1970): 14.

4. Peter Selz and Tom Robbins, "The Pacific Northwest Today," *Art in America* vol. 56 (November/December, 1968): 98.

5. Ibid., 98–101.

6. Lucy Lippard, "Northwest Passage," *Art in America* vol. 64 (July/August 1976): 63.

7. Bill Berkson, "Seattle Site," *Art in America* vol. 74 (July 1986): 68–83+.

8. Bill Berkson, "Report from Seattle: In the Studios," *Art in America* vol. 74 (September 1986): 28.

9. Terry Smith, "The Provincialism Problem," *Artforum* vol. 13 (September 1974): 54–59.

10. Ron Glowen, "Surveying Seattle: A New Image," *Artweek* vol. 14 (November 19, 1983): 1; "A Region Examined," *Artweek* vol. 16 (November 16, 1985): 4; "From the Corner," *Artweek* vol. 26 (December 1995): 5; and "From the Corner," *Artweek* vol. 28 (March 1997): 5.

11. Patricia Failing, "The Pacific Northwest: Sex, Landscape, and Videotape," *Art News* vol. 90 (December 1991): 88–93.

12. Regina Hackett, "Looking beyond Seattle's Glass," *Art and Antiques* vol. 19 (September 1996): 103.

13. Elizabeth Brown and Lisa Corrin, "The Mountain Is Out," *Modern Painters* vol. 15 (Autumn 2002): 48.

14. Herbert Read, *A Concise History of Modern Painting,* rev. ed. (New York and London: Thames and Hudson, Inc., 1991), 252–53; and Serge Guilbaut, *How New York Stole the Idea of Modern Art: Abstract Expressionism, Freedom, and the Cold War* (Chicago and London: The University of Chicago Press, 1983, 1985), 101–65.

Mount Rainier Quotations and Other Historical Commentary Sources:

James Cheholts, "The Mountains," 1927, as told to Thelma Adamson in *Folk-Tales of the Coast Salish,* vol. 27 (New York: The American Folklore Society and G. E. Stechert and Co., Agents, 1934), 268. Reprinted in Astrida R. Blukis Onat, *Tahoma Legends: History in Two Voices,* unpublished manuscript, National Park Service, Seattle, 1999, appendix 6. Judge Elwood Evans, *History of the Pacific Northwest: Oregon and Washington; embracing an account of the original discoveries on the Pacific coast of North America, and a description of the conquest, settlement and subjugation of the original territory of Oregon; also interesting biographies of the earliest settlers and more prominent men and women of the Pacific Northwest, including a description of the climate, soil, productions of Oregon and Washington,* vol. II (Portland, Ore.: North Pacific History Company, 1889), 153. Fitz Hugh Ludlow, *The Heart of the Continent: A Record of Travel across the Plains and in Oregon, with an examination of the Mormon Principle* (New York: Hurd and Houghton, and Cambridge, Mass.: Riverside Press, 1870), 475. John Muir, "Washington and the Puget Sound," from the series *Picturesque California, Oregon, Washington, Alaska, Idaho, Montana, Wyoming, Colorado, Utah, Nevada, Arizona, New Mexico; The Rocky Mountains and the Pacific Slope* part XVII (New York and San Francisco: J. Dewing Publishing Company, 1888): 286–87. Hazard Stevens, *Atlantic Monthly* 38 (November 1876), quoted in *The First Ascent of Takhoma (Rainier),* 2nd ed. (Seattle, Wash.: Shore Publications, 1983), 521. Captain George Vancouver, R.N., "Tuesday, May 8, 1792," *A voyage of discovery to the North Pacific ocean, and round the world; in which the coast of north-west America has been carefully examined and accurately surveyed. Undertaken by His Majesty's command, principally with a view to ascertain the existence of any navigable communication between the North Pacific and North Atlantic oceans; and performed in the years 1790, 1791, 1792, 1793, and 1795, in the Discovery sloop of war, and armed tender Chatham, under the command of Captain George Vancouver,* n.p., quoted in Edmond S. Meany, ed., *Mount Rainier: A Record of Exploration* (New York: The Macmillan Company, 1916), 1. Robert Walkinshaw, *On Puget Sound* (1929; reprint, New York: G. P. Putnam's Sons, 1951), 97–98.

By the latter appellation [Rainier] it was known to all the early settlers up to the time of the completion of the Northern Pacific Railroad to Tacoma. The railroad company then renamed the mountain after the city, claiming that to be the original word designating the place.

The truth of the matter is, however, that the Puyallup Indians, inhabiting the region, called all snowy peaks by the same name,—Tak-ho-ina,—the meaning of which, according to their translation, is "the breast that feeds," meaning to convey the idea that from the eternal snows come the perennial waters of the rivers flowing into the Sound.

Judge Elwood Evans, 1889

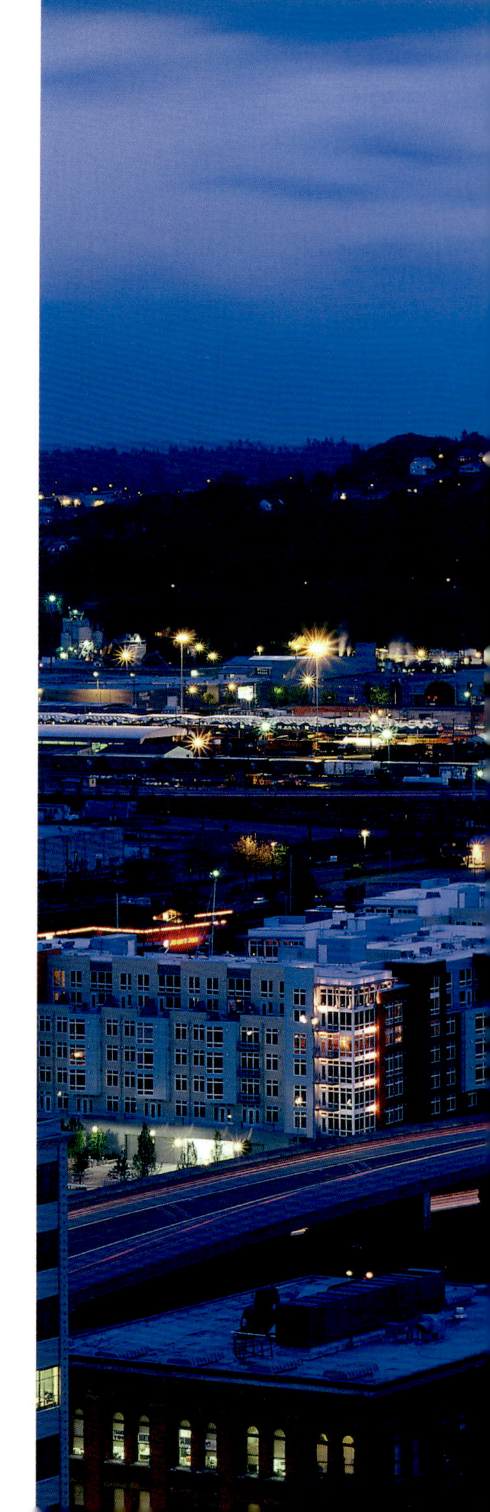

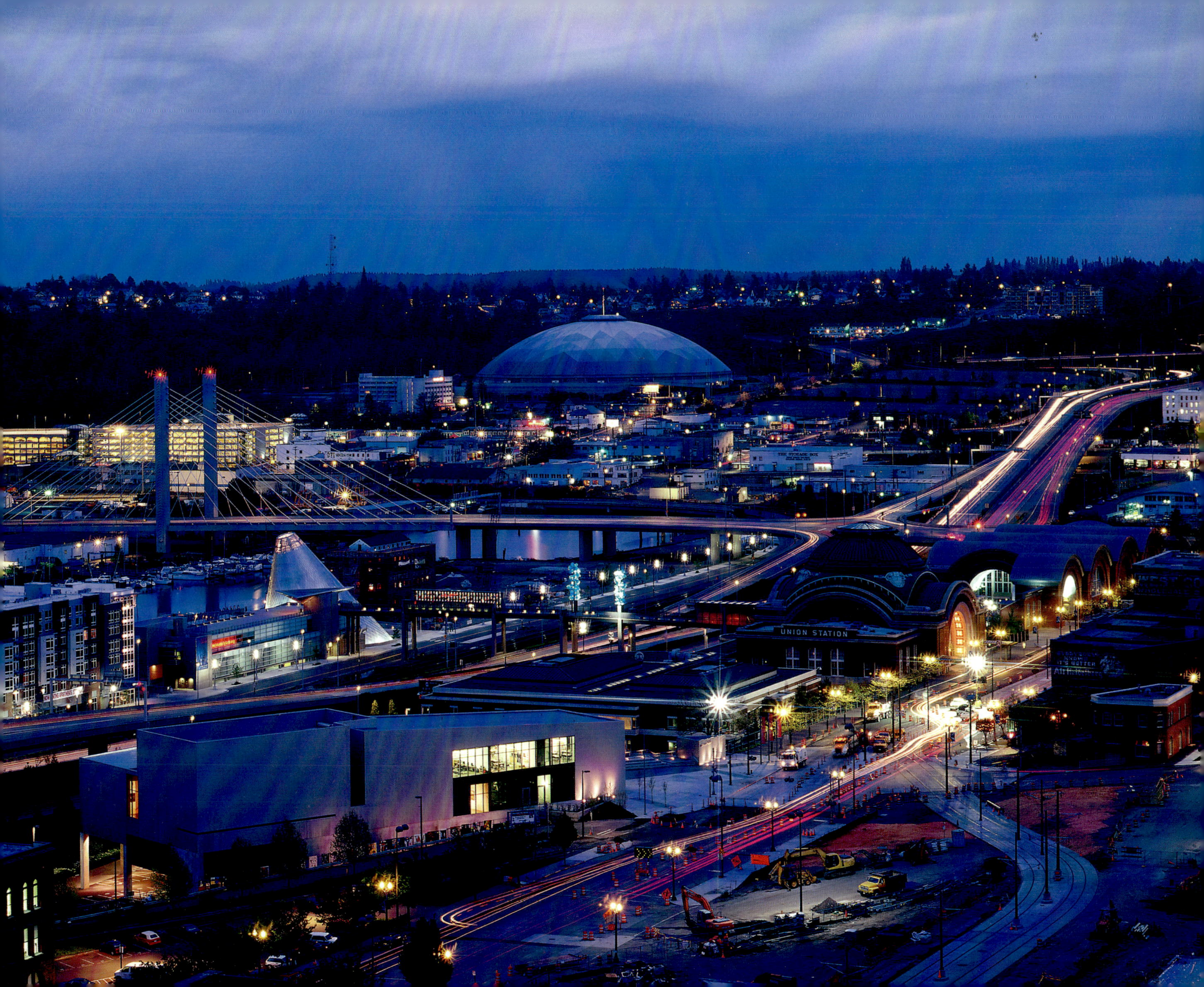

UNION STATION

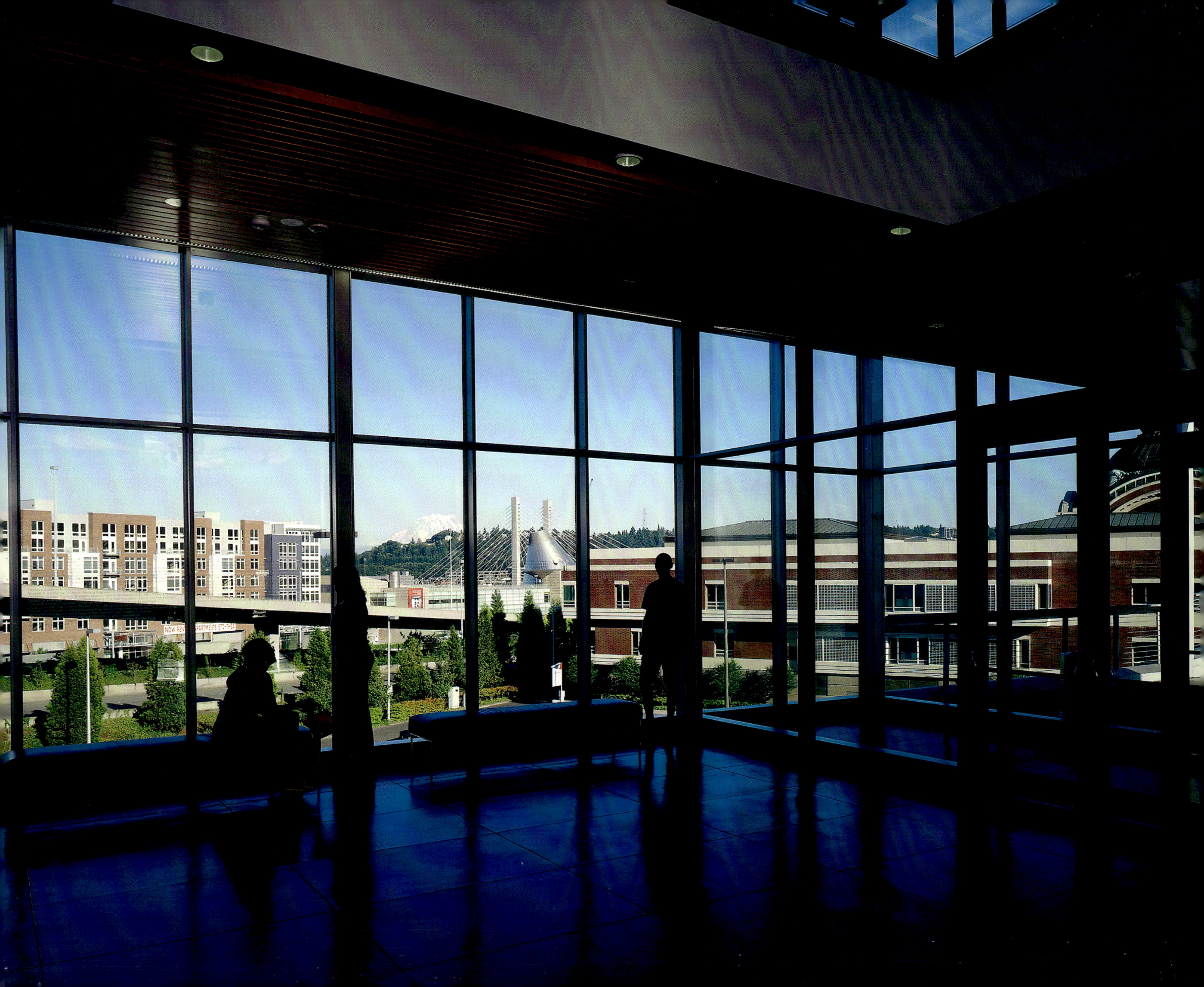

Victoria Adams
(United States, born 1950)
1 *Morning Shimmer,* 2003
Oil on canvas
57 × 70 in.
Tacoma Art Museum, Gift of the artist,
Courtesy of Winston Wächter Fine Art,
Seattle and New York, in honor of
Janeanne A. Upp

Phillip Baldwin
(United States, born 1953)
2 *Untitled custom bracelet,* 2001
Mokumé gané (silver, copper, and
shakudo) on sterling silver
3 × 2 × ½ in.
Tacoma Art Museum, Gift of the artist

Eric Bashor
(United States, born 1975)
3 *Robert Fucci I, II, III, IV, V,* 1999
Oil on canvas on panel
14 × 14 in., each panel
Tacoma Art Museum, Museum
purchase with funds from Mrs. David
Driver and the James D. & Sherry
Raisbeck Foundation

Larry Bemm
(United States, born 1969)
4 *Trial and Error Euthenetics,* 2002
Oil on canvas
41 × 50 in.
Tacoma Art Museum, Gift of the artist,
Courtesy of Kimberly Venardos &
Company, New York

Paul Berger
(United States, born 1951)
5 *Late Fall* from the series *Warp and
Weft: Ground,* 2002
Iris print, artist's proof
35 × 39 in.
Tacoma Art Museum, Gift of the artist

Flora Book
(United States, born 1926)
Millennium Wheel, 2000
Silver and nylon
8¼ in. diam. × 2⅛ in. h.
Tacoma Art Museum, Promised gift
of the artist

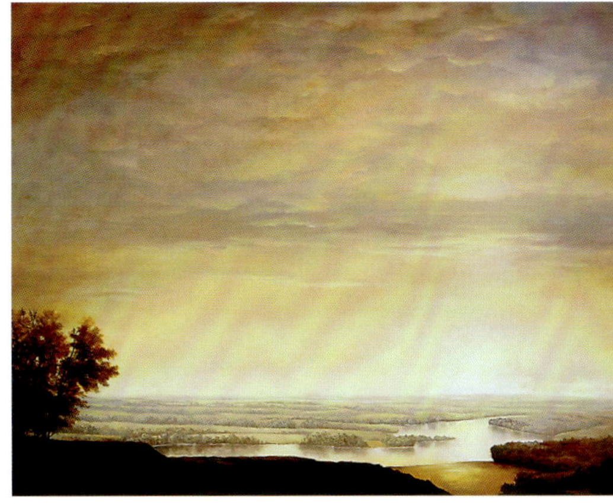

1

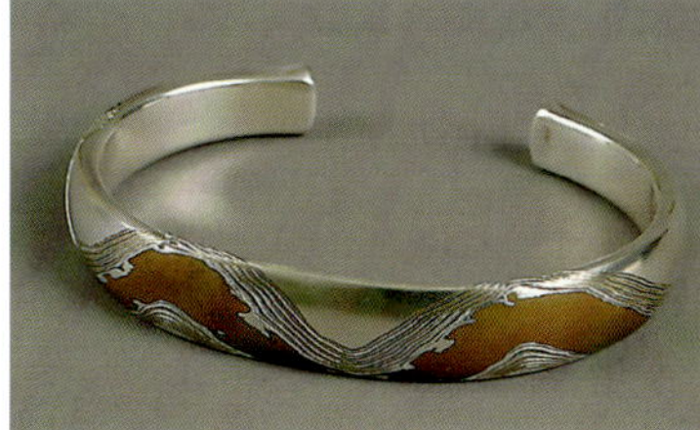

2

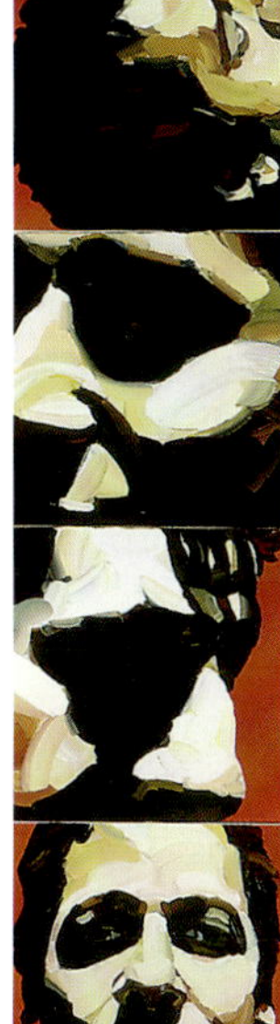

3

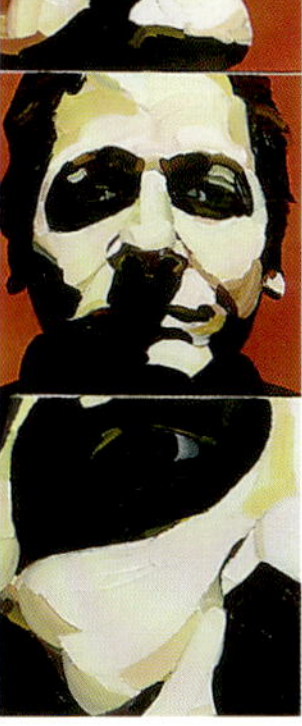

4

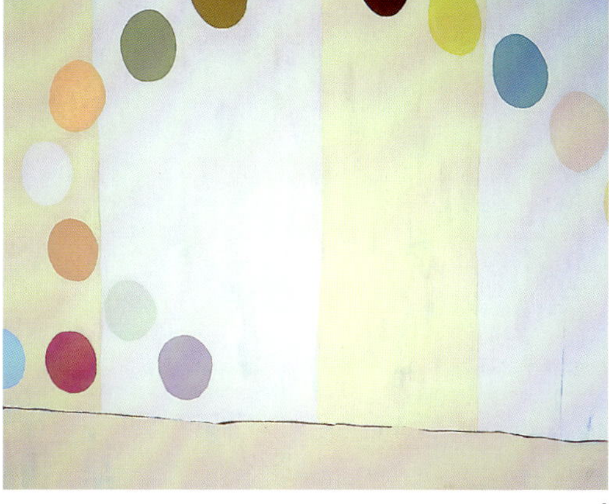

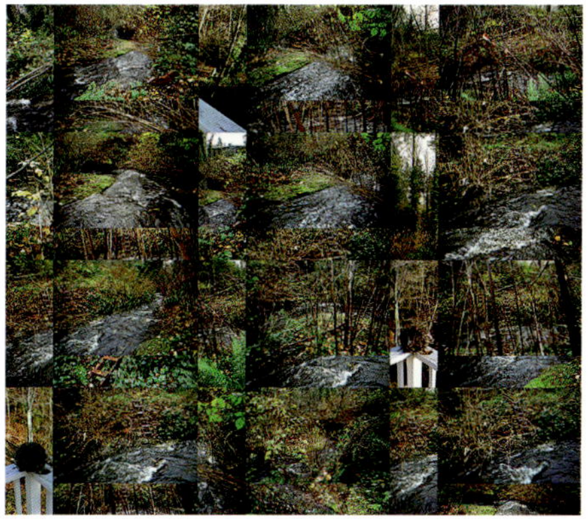

5

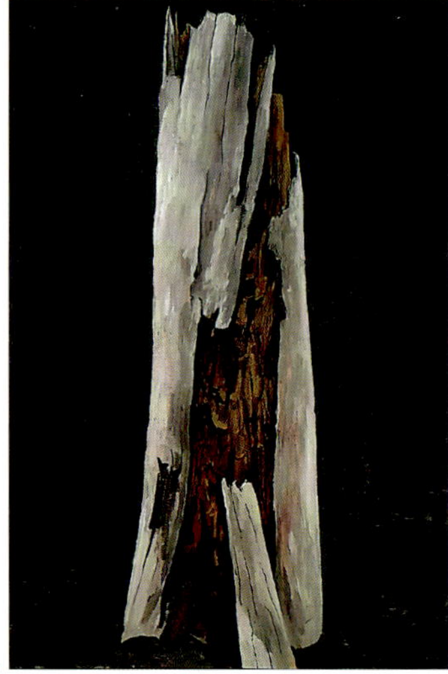

6

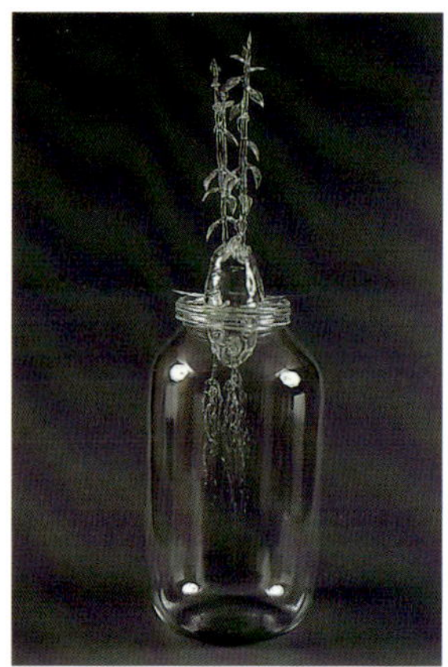

8

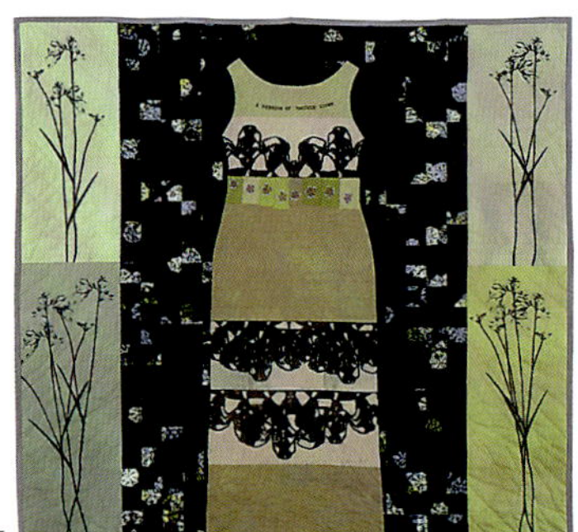

7

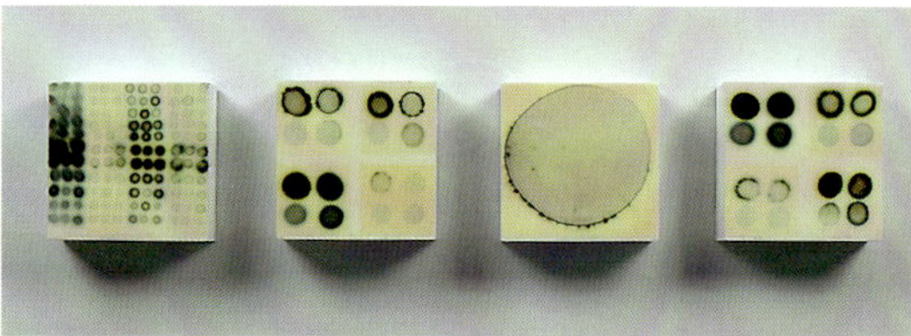

9

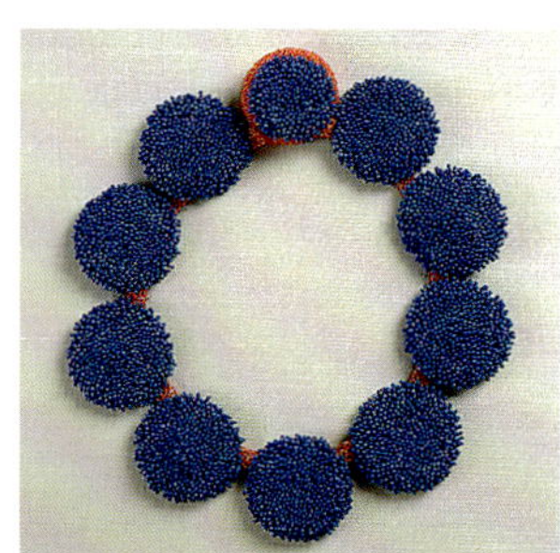

10

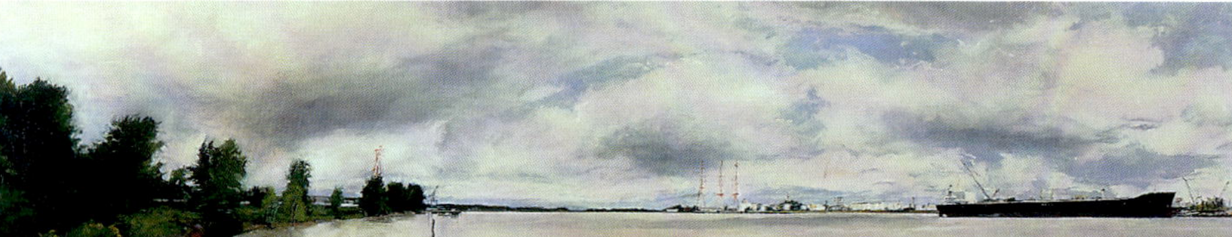

11

Michael Brophy
(United States, born 1960)
6 *Snag I*, 1997
Oil on canvas
91 × 60 in.
Tacoma Art Museum, Gift of the artist
and Laura Russo Gallery, Portland

Rachel Brumer
(United States, born 1956)
7 *Freesias for Madeline*, 2003
Hand quilting, van Dyke printing, and
hand-stamping on cotton and dupioni,
with appliqué, French knots, oil pastel,
and pigment
65 × 67 in.
Tacoma Art Museum, Gift of the
Contemporary QuiltArt Association

Marcia Bruno
(United States, born 1965)
Untitled bracelet from the *Synthetic
Composite Series*, 1995
Acrylic and guitar strings
4½ × 3¾ × 1½ in.
Tacoma Art Museum, Promised gift
of Flora Book

Neckpiece #2 from the *Tension Series*,
2001
Acrylic, steel, and sterling silver
13¼ in. diameter
Tacoma Art Museum, Gift of Mia
McEldowney

John Buck
(United States, born 1946)
8 *Potato*, 1998
Blown and lampworked glass
39½ × 10 × 10 in.
Tacoma Art Museum, Gift of Greg
Kucera and Larry Yocom

Jaq Chartier
(United States, born 1961)
9 *Gray #6*, 2003
Acrylic, stains, and paint on wood
panel, four panels
7 × 37 in. overall
Tacoma Art Museum, Gift of the
William Traver Gallery

David K. Chatt
(United States, born 1960)
10 *Blue Dot Necklace*, 2001
Glass beads and nylon
20¼ in. diam.
Tacoma Art Museum, Promised gift
of Mia McEldowney

Sally Cleveland
(United States, born 1952)
11 *View of the Arco Juneau from the
West Bank*, 1999
Oil on panel
10 × 48 in.
Tacoma Art Museum, Gift of the
artist and Augen Gallery

Andy Cooperman
(United States, born 1958)
Alchemy #1, 1996
Forged and fabricated 14-karat,
18-karat, and 22-karat gold with
sterling squares, ruby, and opal
4¼ × 1⅞ in.
Tacoma Art Museum, Promised gift
of Susan Beech

Suspended Chrysalis, 1997
Fabricated, hot-worked, and forged
shibuichi, 14-karat and 18-karat gold
with opal and ruby
4¼ × 1⅞ in.
Tacoma Art Museum, Promised gift
of Susan Beech

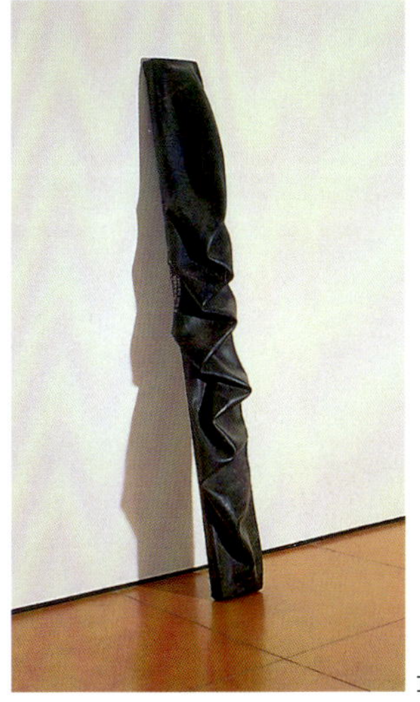
12

Imogen Cunningham
(United States, 1883–1976)

12 *Under the Queensboro Bridge,* 1934
Gelatin silver print
5⁷⁄₁₆ × 6¾ in.
Tacoma Art Museum, Gift of the
Aloha Club

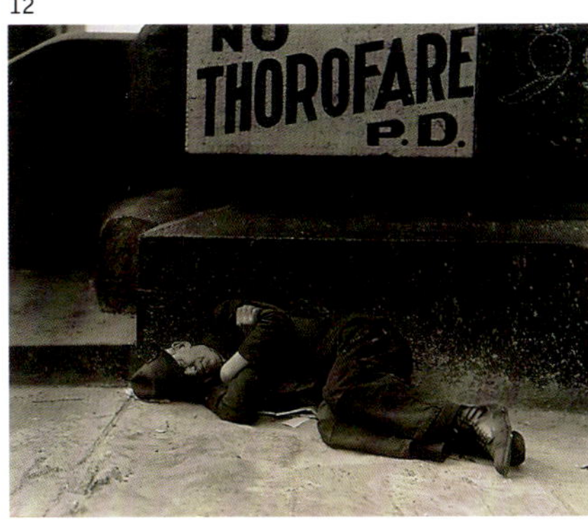

David Darraugh
(United States, born 1952)

13 *Untitled,* 1997
Rubber, wood, and metal
96 × 14 × 11 in.
Tacoma Art Museum, Gift from the
Collection of Edward Albee

13

Marita Dingus
(United States, born 1957)

14 *Mojo Molding,* 2000
Microfiche, photocopies, and Mylar
4½ × 71¼ in. and 3¾ × 35⅞ in.
Tacoma Art Museum, Gift of Carol I.
Bennett

14

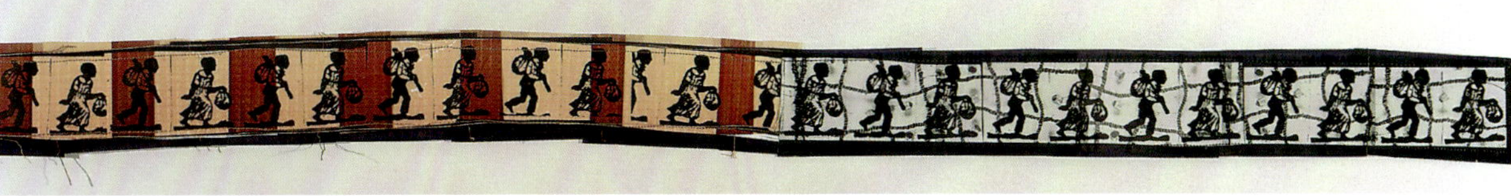

Michael Ehle
(United States, 1953–1999)

15 *Fakir,* 1992
Gouache on rice paper
72 × 36 in.
Tacoma Art Museum, Gift of Greg
Kucera and Larry Yocom

Joe Max Emminger
(United States [birth date unknown])

16 *Our Music,* 2002
Acrylic on paper
43 × 57½ in.
Tacoma Art Museum, Gift of the artist
and Grover/Thurston Gallery

Dennis Evans
(United States, born 1946)

17 *Writing Lessons,* 2002
Mixed media and encaustic on canvas
on board, fifteen panels
84 × 84 in., overall
Tacoma Art Museum, Gift of the artist
and Woodside/Braseth Gallery

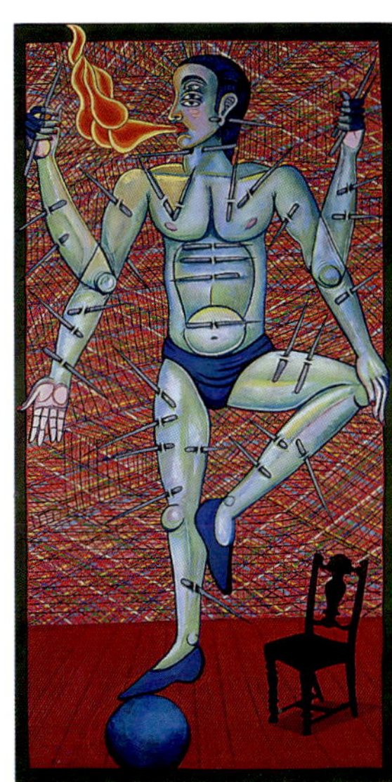
15

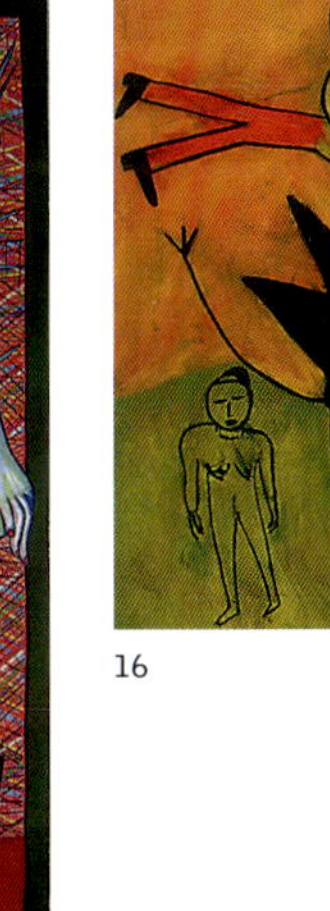

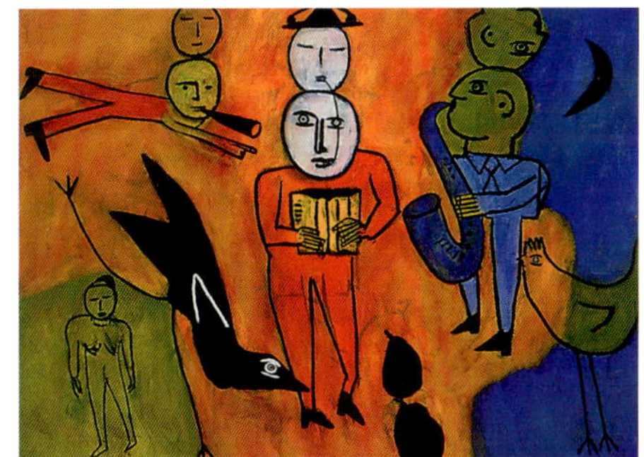
16

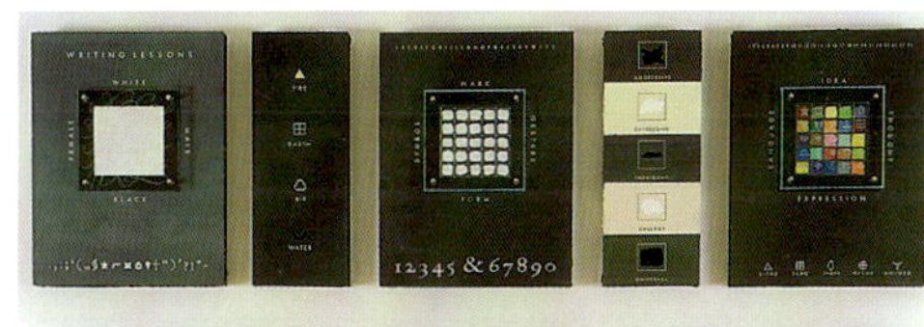

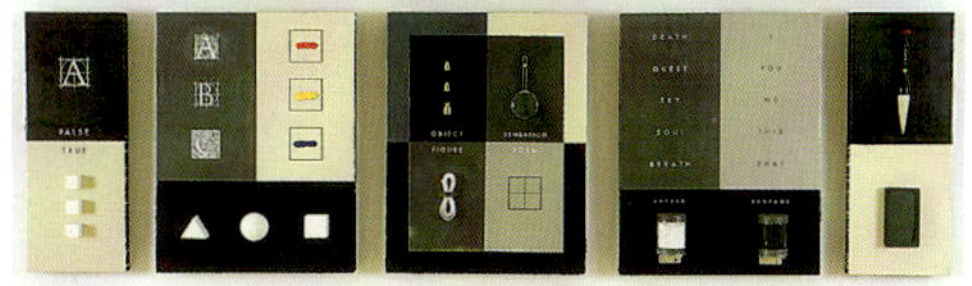

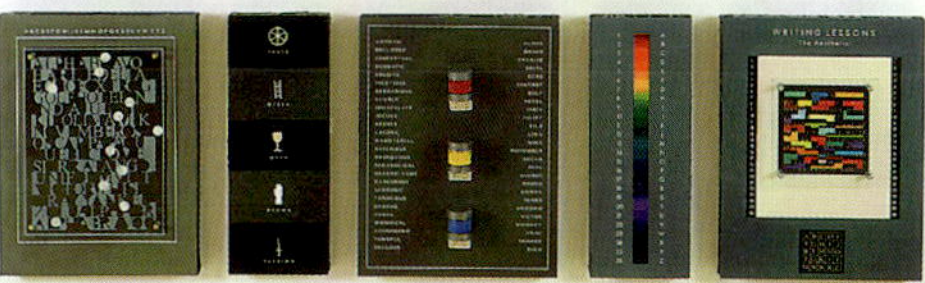
17

18

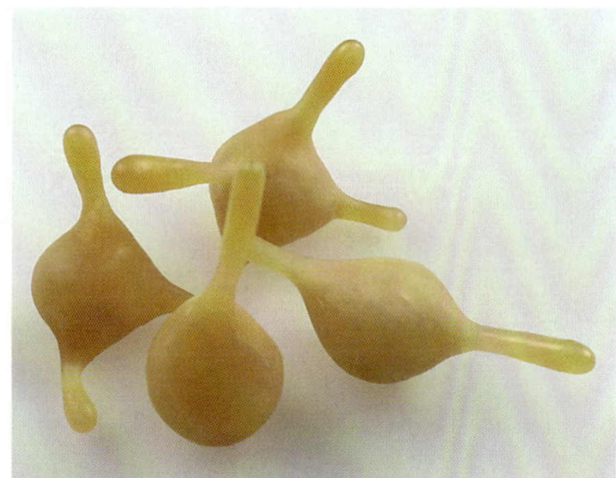

19

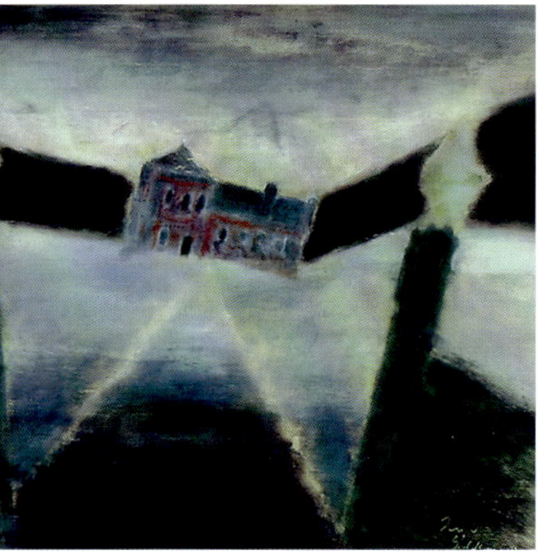

21

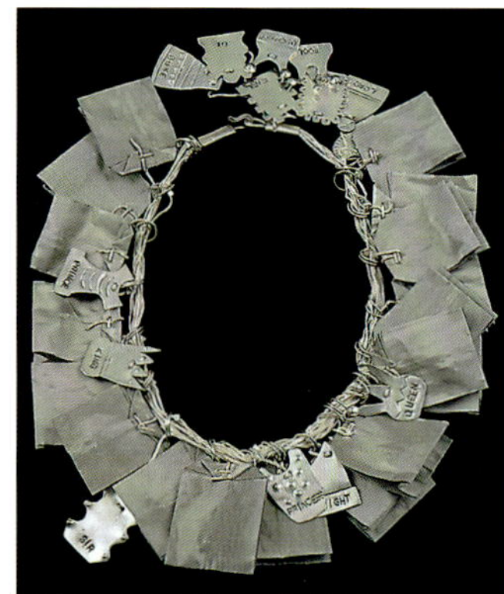

23

20

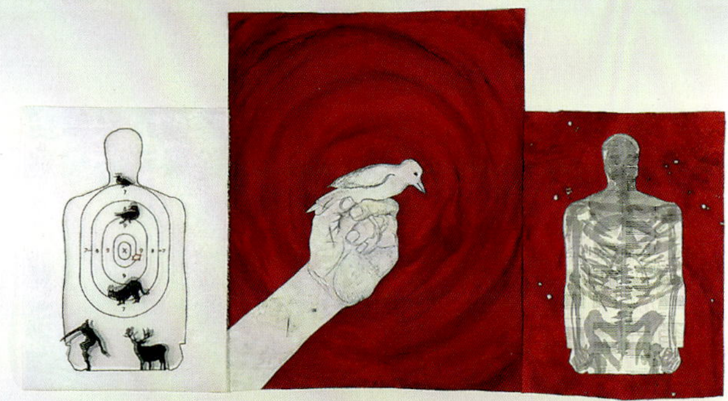

22

Ellen George
(United States, born 1957)
19 *Amber,* 2003
Polymer clay
2 × 1½ × ¾ in.
Tacoma Art Museum, Gift of the
artist and PDX Gallery

Kathryn Glowen
(United States, born 1941)
20 *Dress of Years,* 1997
Child's christening dress, 101 paper
tags with collage, paper collage on
gilded wood, framed mirror, and
vintage photographs by Frank P. Rand
66 × 31 × 7 in.
Tacoma Art Museum, Gift of the artist

Joseph Goldberg
(United States, born 1947)
21 *Black Angel,* 1979
Encaustic on paper
24 × 30 in.
Tacoma Art Museum, Gift of Dr. Dale
Hall and Mrs. Susan Russell Hall

Layne Goldsmith
(United States, born 1950)
22 *Learning to Discern,* 1998
Mixed media on canvas with
reconstructed book and bullet holes,
triptych
67¼ × 124 in.
Tacoma Art Museum, Gift of the artist

Morris Graves
(United States, 1910–2001)
Ferret, 1954
Gouache, ink, and pastel on paper
17¾ × 26⅛ in.
Tacoma Art Museum, Gift of
Jean Roskos in memory of her
husband George Roskos

Sally Finch
(United States, born England 1954)
18 *The Wasteland Revisited I,* 2001
Paper, dye, book text, graphite, and
thread
17 × 17 in.
Tacoma Art Museum, Gift of the artist
and Froelick Gallery, Portland

Laurie Hall
(United States, born 1944)
23 *The Royal Brew Ha Ha!,* 1994
Stainless steel, silver, ink, and
hematite
9 × 9 × 1½ in.
Tacoma Art Museum, Promised gift
of Sharon Campbell

Gaylen Hansen
(United States, born 1921)
24 *Kernal Riding through Snakes,* 1989
Oil on canvas
60½ × 72 in.
Tacoma Art Museum, Museum
purchase and gift of William and
Barbara Street

Alfred Harris
(United States, born Germany, 1953)
25 *Astrud,* 1994
Oil and mixed media on canvas
60 × 60 in.
Tacoma Art Museum, Gift of the artist
and Froelick Gallery, Portland

Randy Hayes
(United States, born 1944)
26 *The Ferry to Eagle Lake,* 2003
Oil on photographs, pushpins
64 × 110 in.
Tacoma Art Museum, Gift of the artist

Stephen Hazel
(United States, born 1928)
27 *The Hero Death Spends Himself upon
Bright Rock,* 1987
Mixed media
41 × 30 in.
Tacoma Art Museum, Gift of the artist

Robert Helm
(United States, born 1943)
Beached Shrub, 1990
Oil on panel
12¼ × 16¼ × 2 in.
Tacoma Art Museum, Gift of Mr. and
Mrs. Robert M. Sarkis

28 *Birds Eye,* 1992
Oil on panel
16 × 12 × 2 in.
Tacoma Art Museum, Gift of Mr. and
Mrs. Robert M. Sarkis

After Petworth I, 1996
Oil on panel
11⅜ × 14⁷⁄₁₆ × 1½ in.
Tacoma Art Museum, Gift of Mr. and
Mrs. Robert M. Sarkis

After Petworth II, 1996
Oil on panel
11⅜ × 14⁷⁄₁₆ × 1½ in.
Tacoma Art Museum, Gift of Mr. and
Mrs. Robert M. Sarkis

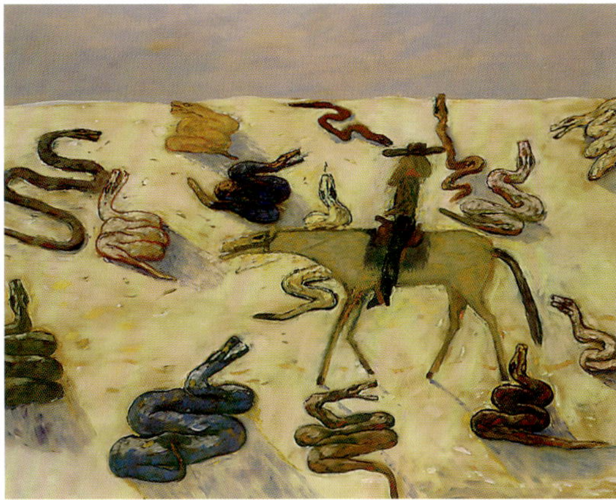

24

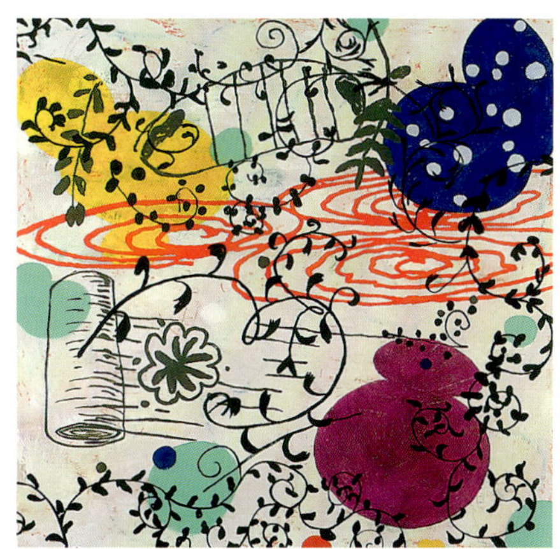

25

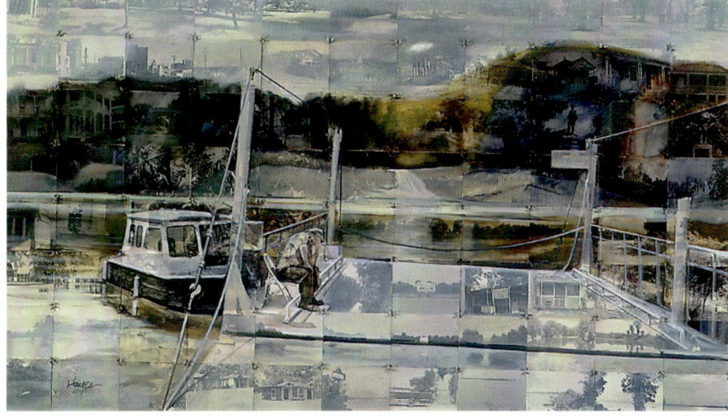

26

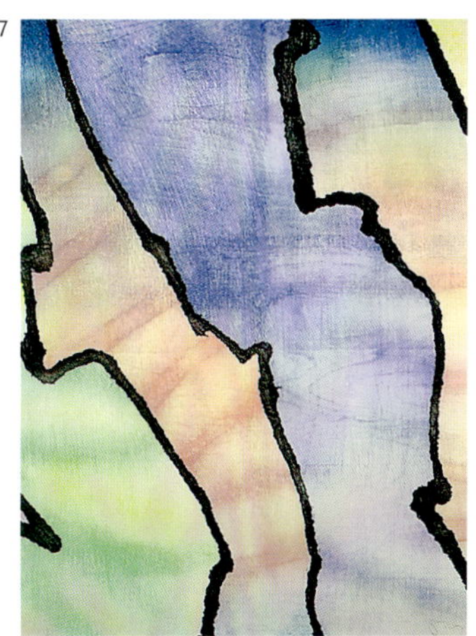

27

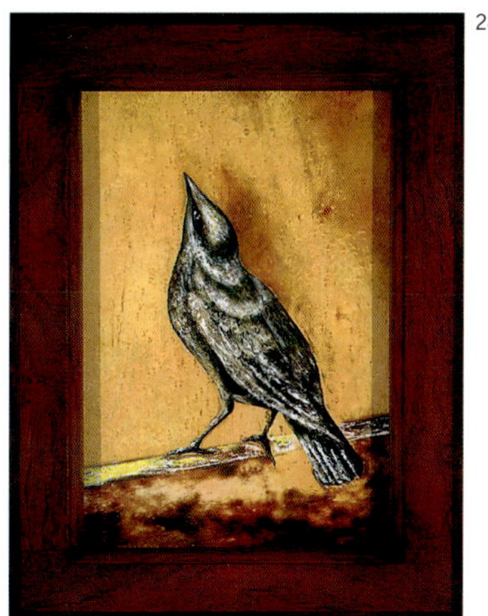

28

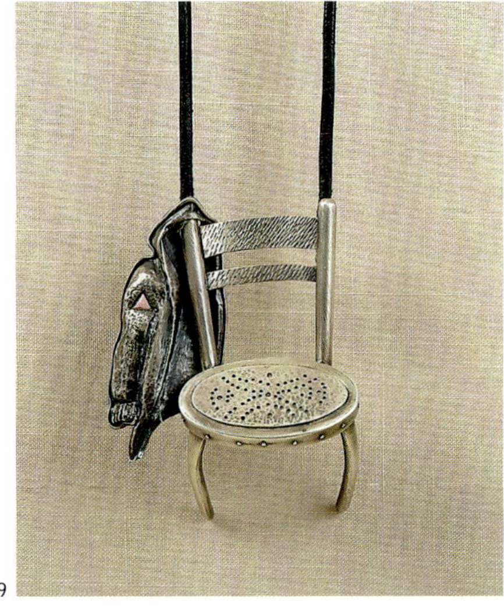

29

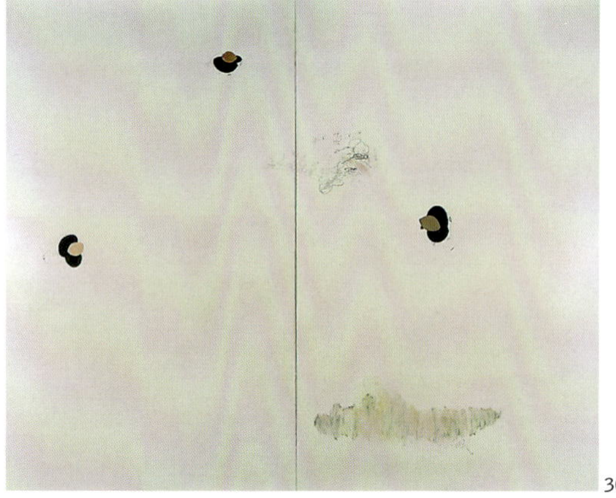

30

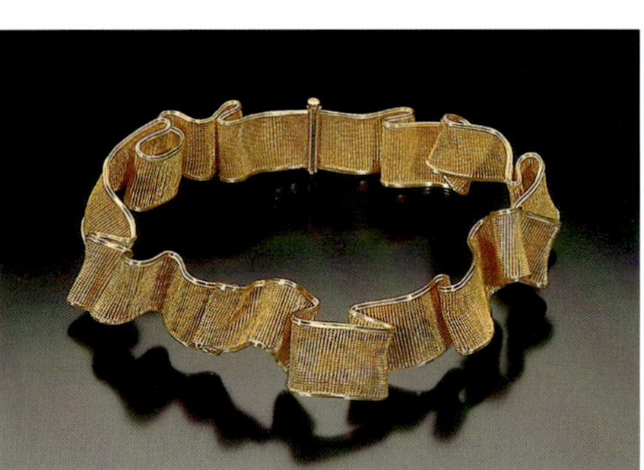

31

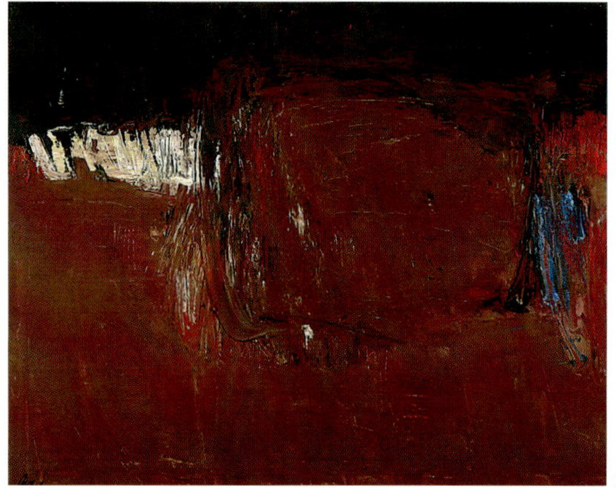

32

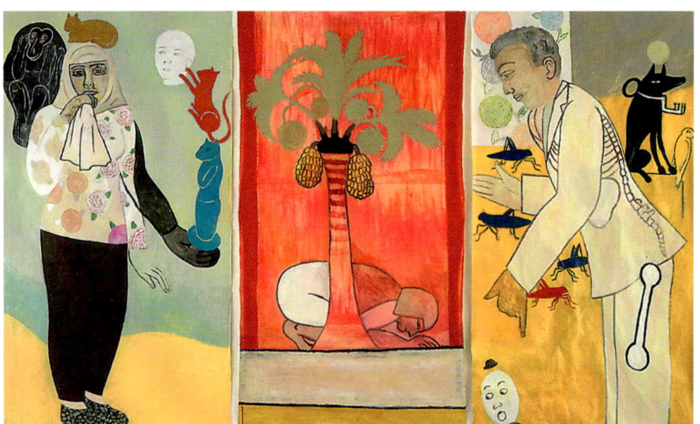

33

Ron Ho
(United States, born 1936)
29 *Vanished Wishes,* 1990
Forged and fabricated silver with
leather and enameling
14 × 2 × 2 in.
Tacoma Art Museum, Promised gift
of Lloyd Herman

Patrick Holderfield
(United States, born 1969)
30 *Untitled (Autumn),* 2001
Pencil, colored pencil, ink, and pastel
on paper
85 × 102½ in.
Tacoma Art Museum, Museum
purchase with funds from Ben and
Aileen Krohn and David Lewis

Mary Lee Hu
(United States, born 1943)
31 *Choker #83,* 2000
22-karat and 18-karat gold
6⅛ × 6¼ × 1 in.
Tacoma Art Museum, Museum
purchase with funds from the Webb-
Roven Foundation, Susan Beech,
Donna Schneier, Friends of Jewelry
at Tacoma Art Museum, Art Jewelry
Forum, and the Ramona Solberg
Endowment

William Ivey
(United States, 1919–1992)
32 *Brown Study,* 1953
Oil on canvas
26 × 32 in.
Tacoma Art Museum, Gift of Dr. Dale
Hall and Mrs. Susan Russell Hall

Fay Jones
(United States, born 1936)
33 *Now and Then (The Guide, The
Builder,* and *The Transfer Man),* 1999
Acrylic, sumi, and collage on paper,
triptych
72¾ × 39 in., each panel
Tacoma Art Museum, Gift of
Carol I. Bennett

Kevin Kadar
(United States, born 1955)
*Figure 834 (Susan at Hipbone
Studios),* 2001
Oil on gessoed wood panel
12⅛ × 16⅛ in.
Tacoma Art Museum, Gift of the artist
and Froelick Gallery, Portland

34 *Figure 850 (Susan at P.S.U.),* 2002
Oil on gessoed museum board
8⅝ × 8⅝ in.
Tacoma Art Museum, Gift of the artist
and Froelick Gallery, Portland

Howard Kottler
(United States, 1930–89)
35 *Swiss Miss,* 1973
Glazed ceramic and Plexiglas
13 × 12 × 8 in.
Tacoma Art Museum, Gift of William
Calderhead

Keith Lewis
(United States, born 1959)
36 *Of Rarity Untold (Scene from an
Imaginary Libretto by Ronald
Firbank),* 1997
Sterling silver, copper, enamel on
fine silver
2⅛ × 2⅛ × ⅝ in.
Tacoma Art Museum, Promised gift
of Sharon Campbell

Micki Lippe
(United States, born 1943)
Spirit House, ca. 2002
Sterling silver and gold foil
3⅛ × 1 × ¾ in.
Tacoma Art Museum, Promised gift
of Flora Book

Victor Maldonado
(United States, born Mexico 1976)
37 *Cross Road,* 2002
Hand stamped ink on paper
23 × 30 in.
Tacoma Art Museum, Gift of the artist
and Froelick Gallery, Portland

34
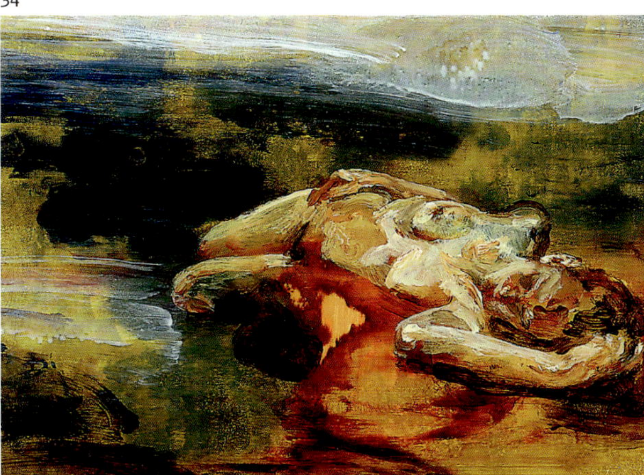

35
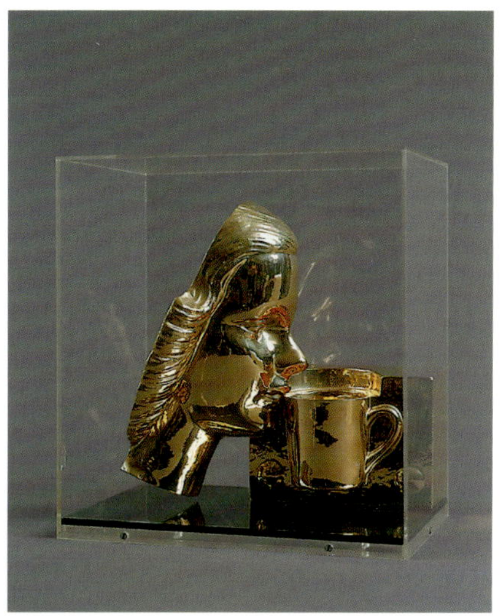

36
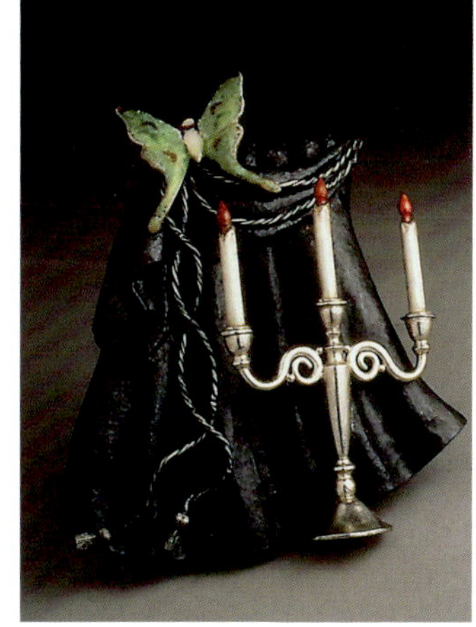

37
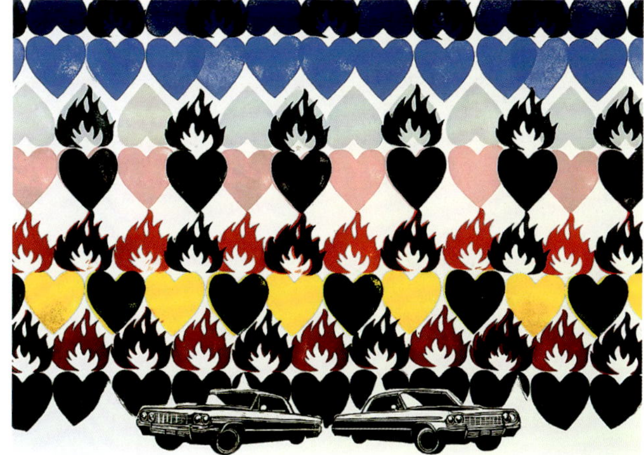

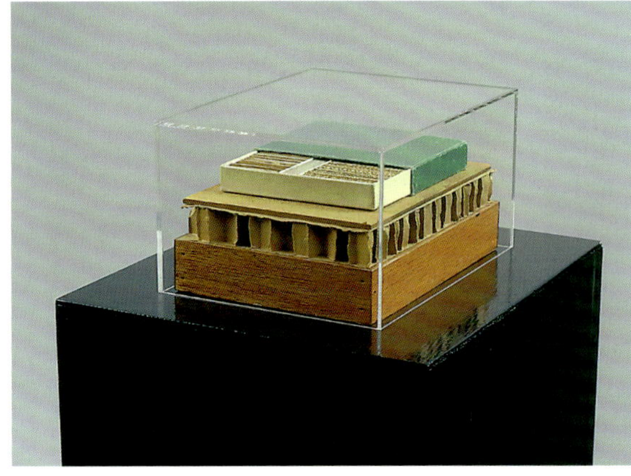

38

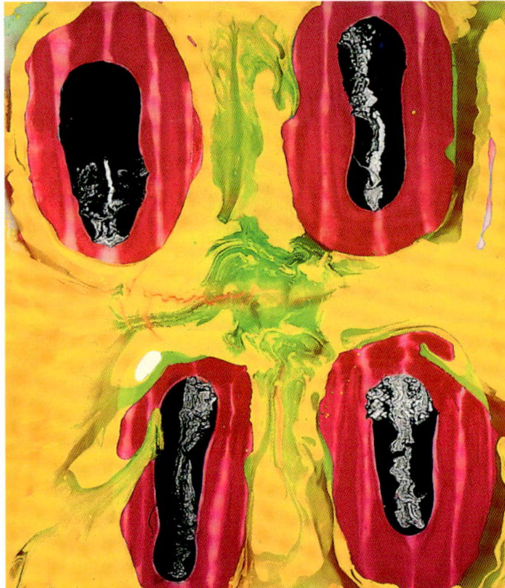

40

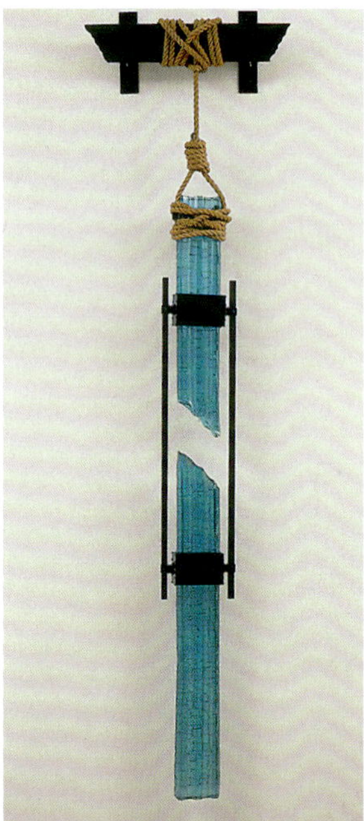

39

41

D. E. May
(United States, born 1952)
38 *Untitled,* 2002
Mixed media
6¼ × 8⅛ × 3 in.
Tacoma Art Museum, Gift of the
artist and PDX Gallery

Nancy Mee
(United States, born 1951)
39 *Hanging and Bound Spine* from
The Justice Series, 1997
Glass, steel, and rope
94 × 12 × 4 in.
Tacoma Art Museum, Gift of the
artist and Woodside/Braseth Gallery

Mark Takamichi Miller
(United States, born 1960)
40 *Untitled,* 1999
Acrylic on canvas
72 × 64 in.
Tacoma Art Museum, Gift of
Ben and Aileen Krohn

Tom Miller
(United States, born 1943)
Mogollon, 1988
Gelatin silver print
13¼ × 17¼ in.
Tacoma Art Museum, Gift of the
artist and Augen Gallery, Portland

41 *Heart,* 1995
Gelatin silver print
15¹⁵⁄₁₆ × 19⅞ in.
Tacoma Art Museum, Gift of the
artist and Augen Gallery, Portland

Braid, 1996
Gelatin silver print
13⅝ × 17⅛ in.
Tacoma Art Museum, Gift of the
artist and Augen Gallery, Portland

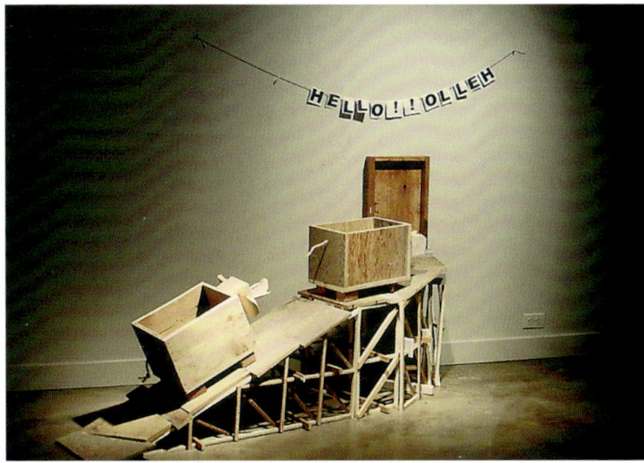

42

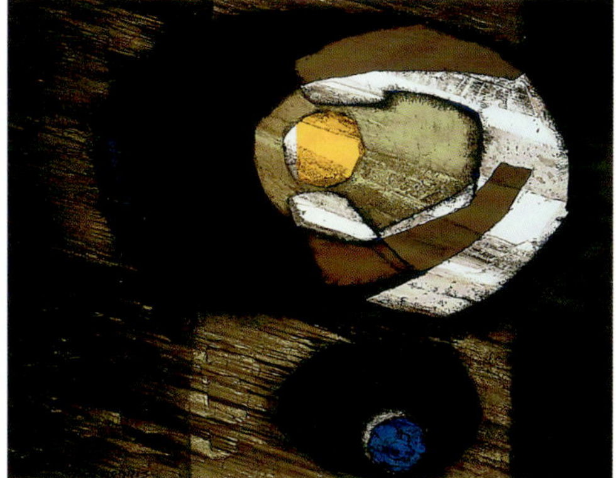

43

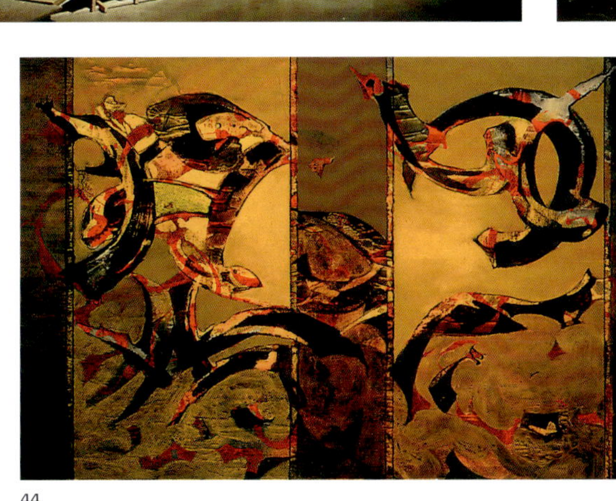

44

45

Jeffry Mitchell
(United States, born 1958)
42 *Hello! Hello!,* 2002
Wood, nails, paper, and string
53 × 84 × 41 in.
Tacoma Art Museum, Gift of
Michael Klein in memory of his
parents Hedy and Emil Klein

Carl Morris
(United States, 1911–1993)
43 *Untitled,* 1971
Oil on canvas
58½ × 71½ in.
Tacoma Art Museum, Gift of
Herbert and Lucia Pruzan

Tuscany Stone, 1972
Tempera on paper
20¼ × 27¼ in.
Tacoma Art Museum, Gift of the
Carl and Hilda Morris Foundation

Tuscany Stone, 1972
Tempera on paper
20¼ × 27⅜ in.
Tacoma Art Museum, Gift of the
Carl and Hilda Morris Foundation

Tuscany Stone, 1972
Tempera on paper
27⅜ × 30¼ in.
Tacoma Art Museum, Gift of the
Carl and Hilda Morris Foundation

Tuscany Stone, 1972
Tempera on paper
20¼ × 27⅜ in.
Tacoma Art Museum, Gift of the
Carl and Hilda Morris Foundation

44 *Calligraphy,* 1985
Acrylic on canvas
50 × 72 in.
Tacoma Art Museum, Gift of the
Carl and Hilda Morris Foundation

Megan Murphy
(United States, born 1969)
45 *Reflection,* 2002
Oil on glass
42 × 29 × ¼ in.
Tacoma Art Museum, Gift of the
artist and PDX Gallery

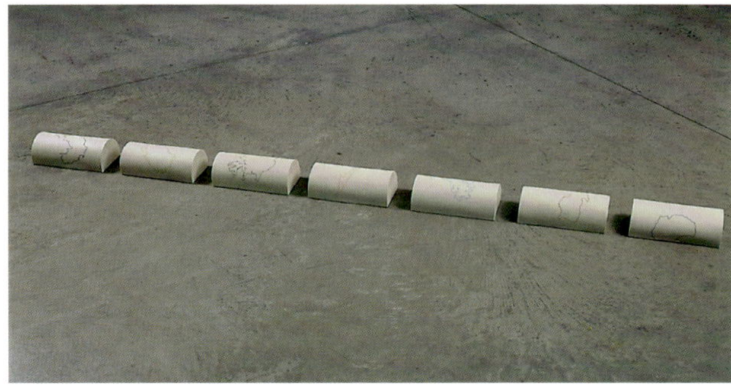

46

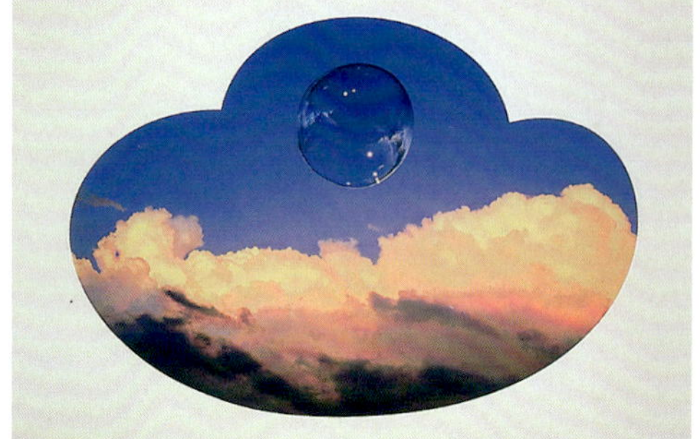

48

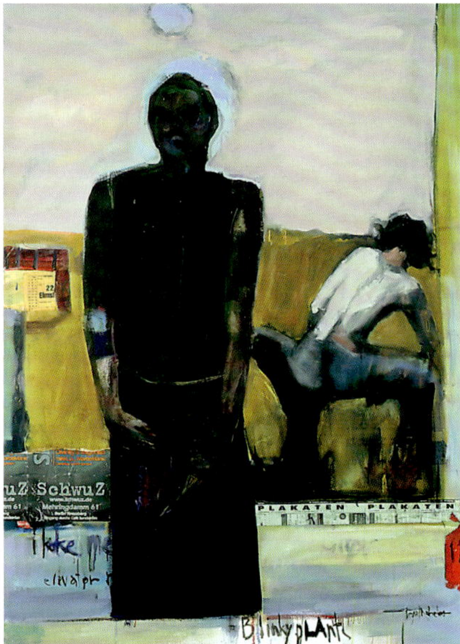

47

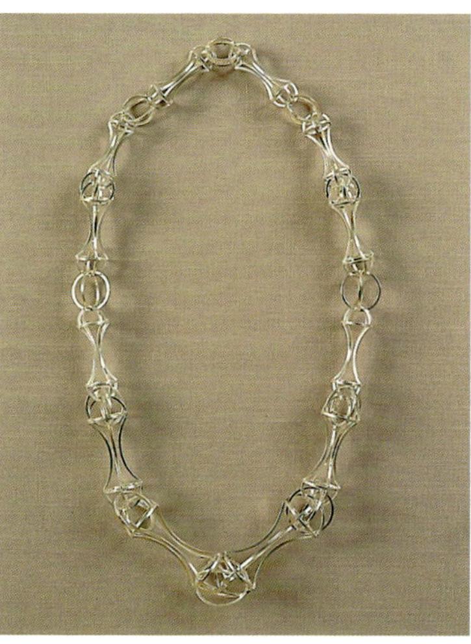

49

Yuki Nakamura
(Japan, born 1971)
46 *Island Pillows,* 2003
Porcelain, seven components
5½ × 91½ × 3½ in., overall
Tacoma Art Museum, Gift of the
artist and David Lewis in honor
of Kent Lewis and Claire Eileen
Osband-Lewis

Royal Nebeker
(United States, born 1945)
47 *Blinky Plants,* 2001
Oil on canvas with collage
70¼ × 50¼ × 1⅛ in.
Tacoma Art Museum, Gift of the
Augen Gallery, Portland

Dream Room, 2001
Oil on canvas with collage
66½ × 54¼ × 1⅛ in.
Tacoma Art Museum, Gift of the
Augen Gallery, Portland

Barbara Noah
(United States, born 1949)
Rise and Fall, 1999
Etching and pencil on paper
18⅝ × 14⅝ in.
Tacoma Art Museum, Gift of the artist

48 *Pop,* 2001
Inkjet print
19⅞ × 28¼ in.
Tacoma Art Museum, Gift of the artist

Gina Pankowski
(United States, born 1965)
49 *Vertebrae #5,* 1996
Sterling silver
30 in. diam.
Tacoma Art Museum, Promised gift
of Mia McEldowney

Joseph Park
(United States, born Canada 1964)
50 *Chess,* 2001
Oil on canvas
20 × 24 in.
Tacoma Art Museum, Gift of David
Lewis in honor of Clinton Williams,
Donald Williams, Eileen Lewis and
Jane Ramm

William Park
(United States, born 1945)
51 *Mathew's Beach,* 2001
Oil on canvas
48 × 52⅛ in.
Tacoma Art Museum, Gift of the
artist and Augen Gallery, Portland

Maria Phillips
(United States, born 1963)
52 *Continuation,* 2001
Sterling silver, copper, and mixed
media
27½ × 5¾ × 2 in.
Tacoma Art Museum, Promised gift
of Donna Briskin

Danny Pierce
(United States, born 1920)
53 *The Jam,* 1985
Oil on canvas
39½ × 49⅞ in.
Tacoma Art Museum, Gift of
Dr. George Berg in memory of
Nancy A. Wynstra

Kathleen Rabel
(United States, born 1943)
54 *Soft-Set,* 2001
Mixed media
52 × 75 in.
Tacoma Art Museum, Gift of the artist

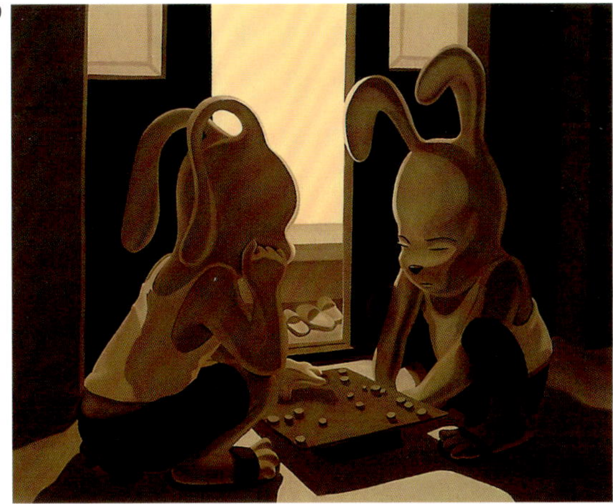

50

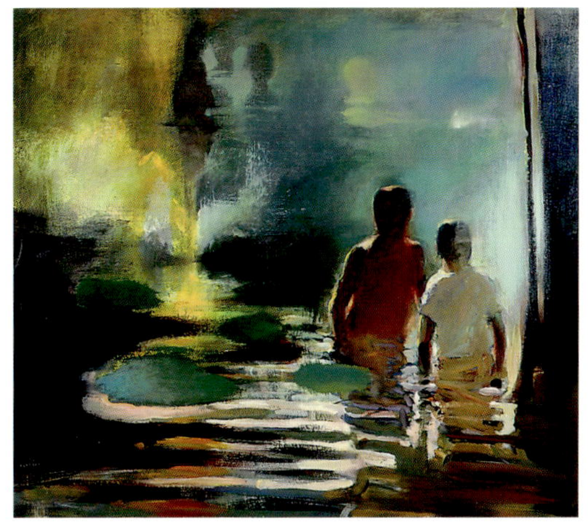

51

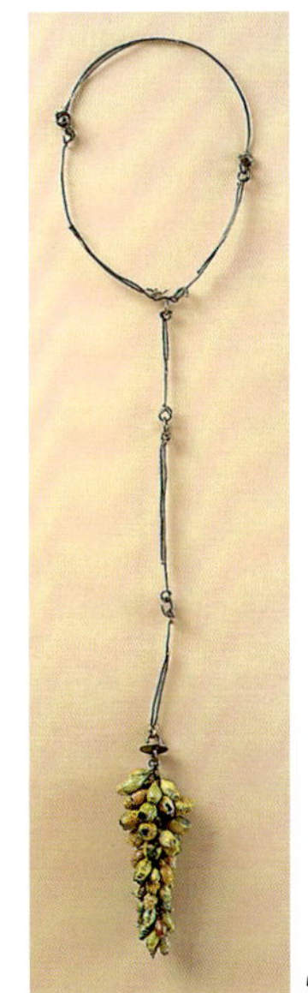

52

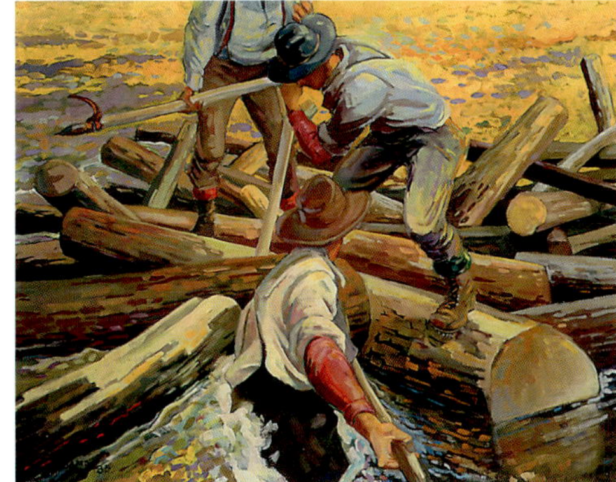

53

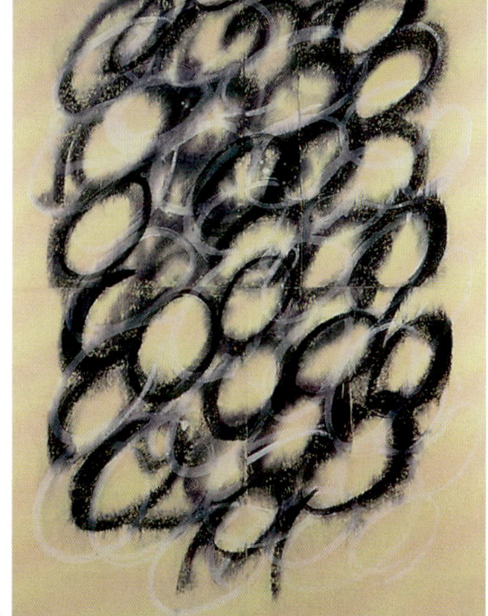

54

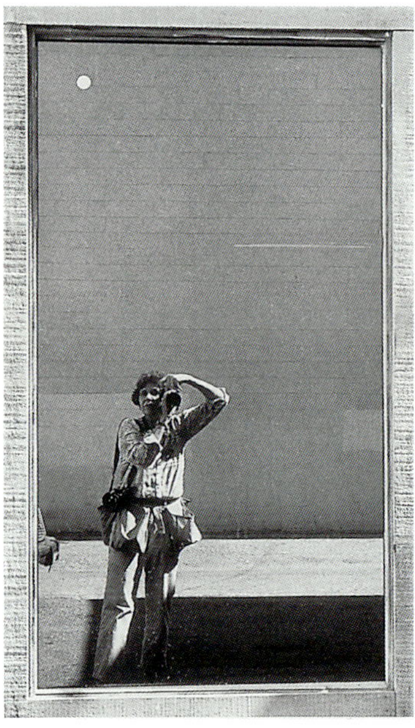

55

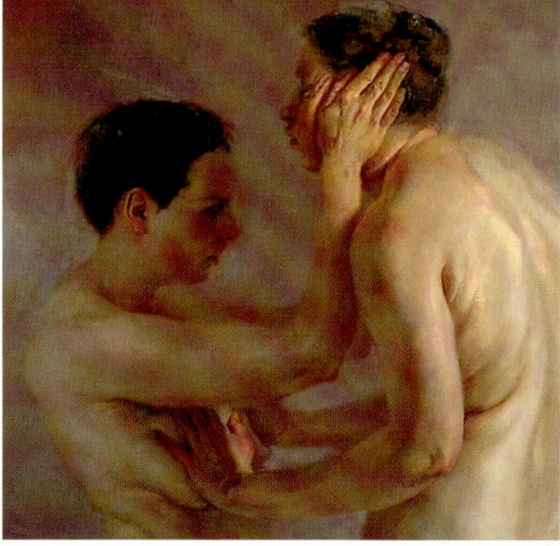

56

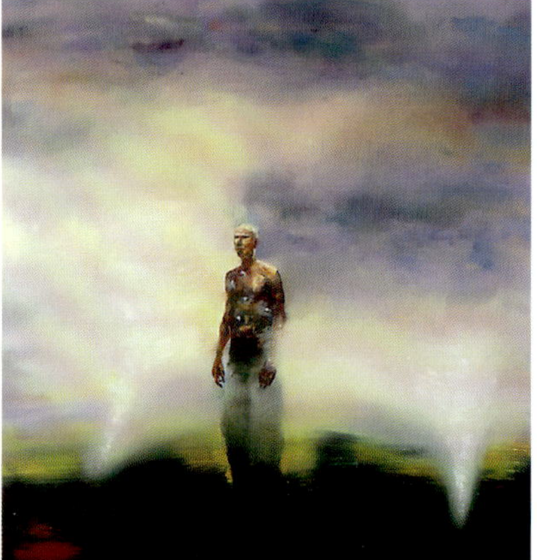

57

Mary Randlett
(United States, born 1924)
Morris Graves, 1949, reprinted 2002
Gelatin silver print
10½ × 10½ in.
Tacoma Art Museum, Gift of the
Aloha Club

Kenneth Callahan, 1964, reprinted
2002
Gelatin silver print
10⅜ × 10¼ in.
Tacoma Art Museum, Gift of the
Aloha Club

William Cumming, 1964, reprinted
2002
Gelatin silver print
12⅛ × 9 in.
Tacoma Art Museum, Gift of the
Aloha Club

Imogen Cunningham, 1965, reprinted
2002
Gelatin silver print
7 × 6¾ in.
Tacoma Art Museum, Gift of the
Aloha Club

Paul Horiuchi, 1966, reprinted 2002
Gelatin silver print
9¼ × 9⅜ in.
Tacoma Art Museum, Gift of the
Aloha Club

William Ivey, 1966, reprinted 2002
Gelatin silver print
15¼ × 15⅛ in.
Tacoma Art Museum, Gift of the
Aloha Club

Carl and Hilda Morris, 1967,
reprinted 2002
Gelatin silver print
8 × 10¼ in.
Tacoma Art Museum, Gift of the
Aloha Club

Frank Okada, 1968, reprinted 2002
Gelatin silver print
9⅛ × 9⅞ in.
Tacoma Art Museum, Gift of the
Aloha Club

Ruth Nomura, 1970, reprinted 2002
Gelatin silver print
7½ × 9¼ in.
Tacoma Art Museum, Gift of the
Aloha Club

Mike Spafford, 1972, reprinted 2002
Gelatin silver print
13¼ × 10¼ in.
Tacoma Art Museum, Gift of the
Aloha Club

Jacob Lawrence, 1983,
reprinted 2002
Gelatin silver print
10¼ × 10½ in.
Tacoma Art Museum, Gift of the
Aloha Club

55 *Mary Randlett,* 1988, reprinted 2002
Gelatin silver print
9⅛ × 5¼ in.
Tacoma Art Museum, Gift of the
Aloha Club

Guy Anderson, 1990, reprinted 2002
Gelatin silver print
10½ × 10¼ in.
Tacoma Art Museum, Gift of the
Aloha Club

Margaret Tomkins, 1990,
reprinted 2002
Gelatin silver print
9¼ × 9½ in.
Tacoma Art Museum, Gift of the
Aloha Club

Johsel Namkung, 2000,
reprinted 2002
Gelatin silver print
6¾ × 9⅞ in.
Tacoma Art Museum, Gift of the
Aloha Club

Hanneline Røgeberg
(United States, born Norway 1963)
56 *Organmachine,* 1998
Oil on canvas
36 × 36 in.
Tacoma Art Museum, Promised
gift of Dr. Jerry Slipman and
Dr. Chet Robachinski

Laura Ross-Paul
(United States, born 1950)
57 *Holes,* 1999
Oil and wax on canvas
55 × 49¼ in.
Tacoma Art Museum, Gift of the
artist and Froelick Gallery, Portland

Michele Russo
(United States, born 1909)
58 *Brown Nude*, 1960
Oil on canvas
57¼ × 47¾ in.
Tacoma Art Museum, Gift of
Herbert and Lucia Pruzan

Susan Seubert
(United States, born 1970)
59 *Lewis and Clark State Park* from the
series *10 Most Popular Places to
Dump a Body in the Columbia River
Gorge,* 1998
Gelatin silver print, artist's proof
from an edition of 10
16 × 20 in.
Tacoma Art Museum, Gift of the
artist and Froelick Gallery, Portland

Mike Shea
(United States, born 1970)
60 *And Neck*, 2000
Lithograph, no. 5 from an edition of 7
23¾ × 22¼ in.
Tacoma Art Museum, Gift of the
artist and Froelick Gallery, Portland

61 *Neck and,* 2000
Lithograph, no. 5 from an edition of 7
23¾ × 22⅛ in.
Tacoma Art Museum, Gift of the
artist and Froelick Gallery, Portland

62 *Reel,* 2000
Lithograph, no. 5 from an edition of 7
23¾ × 22⅛ in.
Tacoma Art Museum, Gift of the
artist and Froelick Gallery, Portland

Roger Shimomura
(United States, born 1939)
63 *Minidoka No. 5 (442ⁿᵈ),* 1979
Acrylic on canvas
60 × 72 in.
Tacoma Art Museum, Gift of
Kim and George Suyama

David Shratter
(United States, born 1953)
64 *Duet V* from the *Onion Series,* 2002
Oil on canvas
19¼ × 17 in.
Tacoma Art Museum, Gift of the
artist and PDX Gallery

58 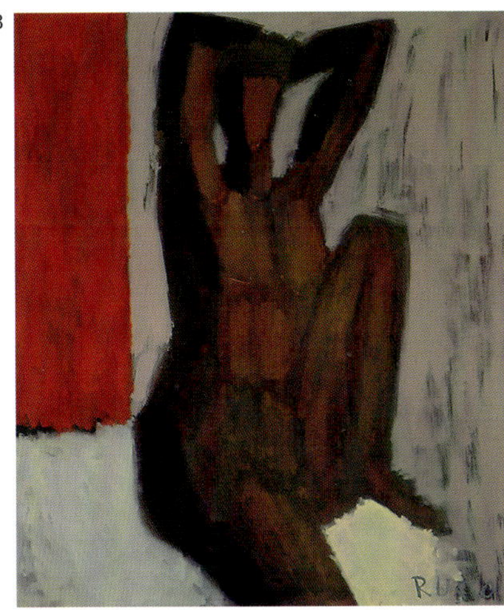

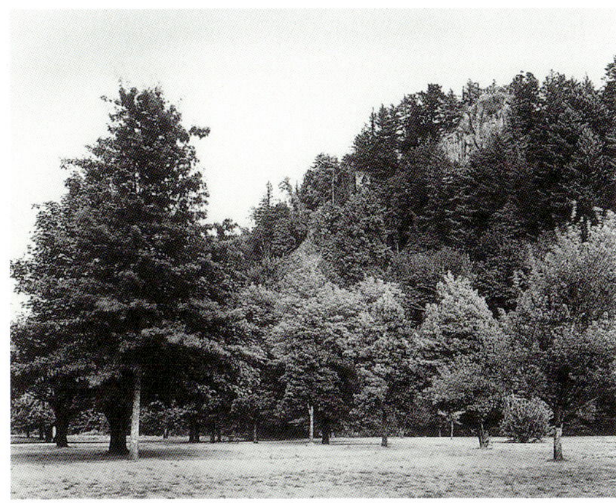
59

61 62 60 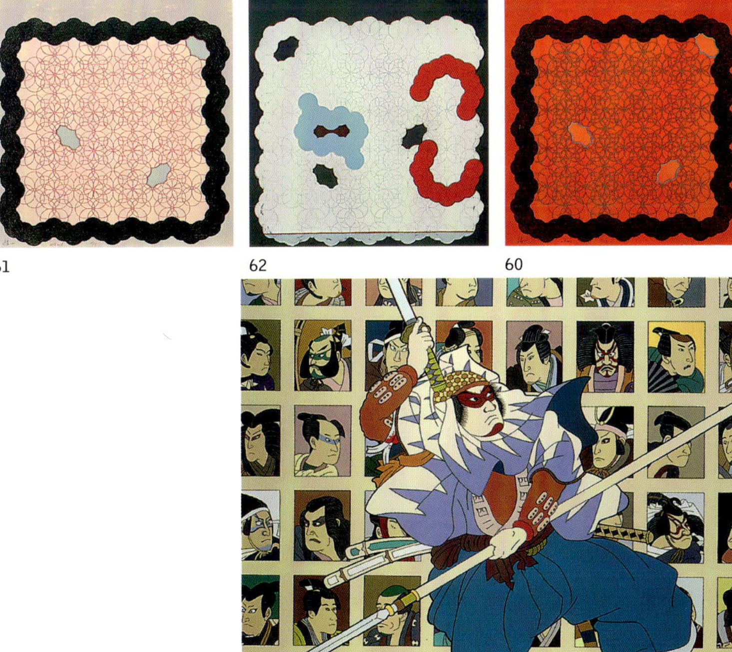

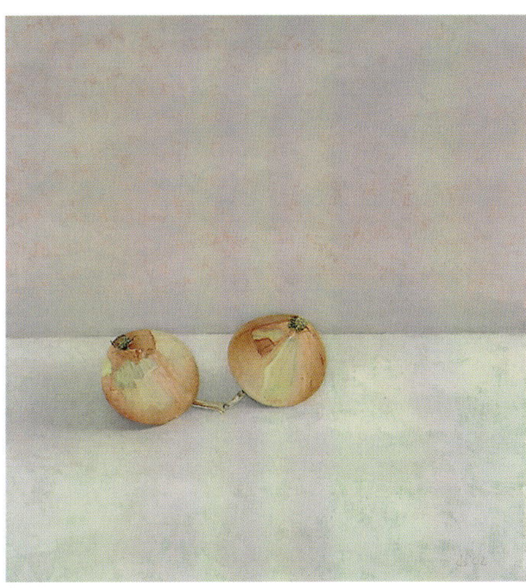
64

63

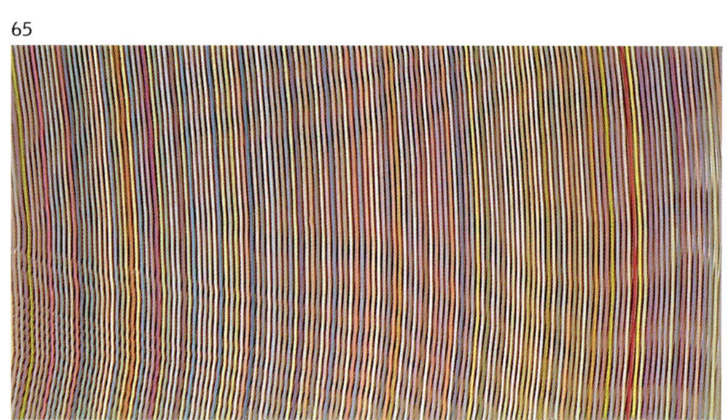

65

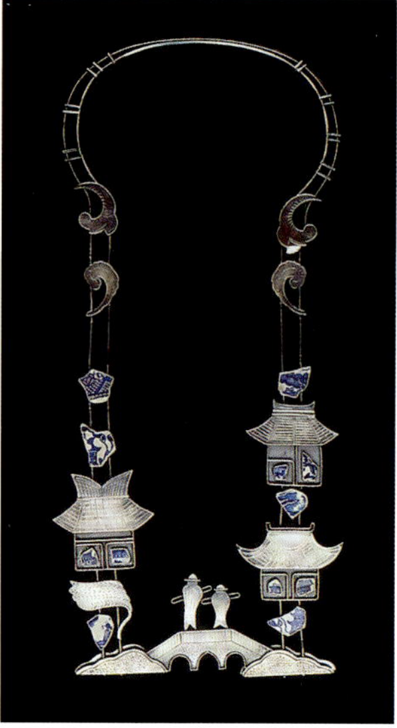

66

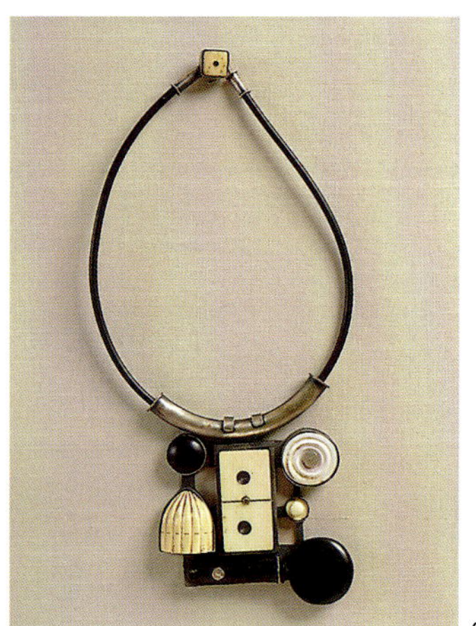

67

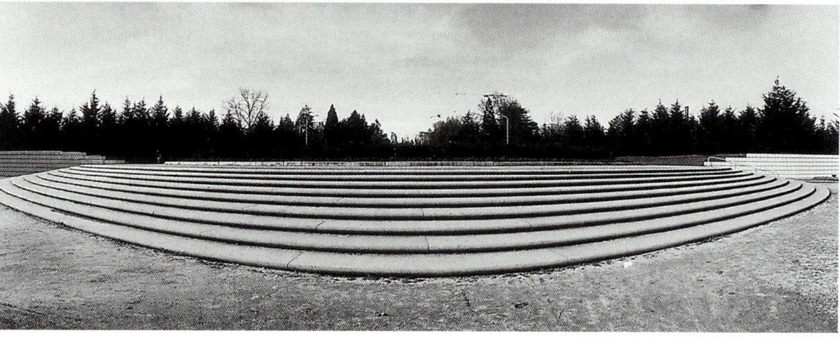

68

Jeffrey Simmons
(United States, born 1968)
65 *Flux,* 2002
Alkyd, Mylar, and epoxy resin on
canvas over wood panel
18 × 33 in.
Tacoma Art Museum, Gift of David
Lewis in honor of Dr. Gregory Lewis,
Nancy Cole, and Delbert Lewis

Kiff Slemmons
(United States, born 1944)
66 *Willow Wear,* 1991
Silver and china shards
16½ × 7⅛ × ¼ in.
Tacoma Art Museum, Promised gift
of Flora Book

Ramona Solberg
(United States, born 1921)
67 *Playing Around,* 2001
Silver, found objects, ivory, and shell
13¼ × 5 × 1 in.
Tacoma Art Museum, Promised gift
of Mia McEldowney

Christian Staub
(United States, born Switzerland
1918)
*Opening in the Modern Art Pavilion
at the Exhibition "Richard Avedon,"*
1974
Gelatin silver print
6 × 14 in.
Tacoma Art Museum, Gift of the artist

Seattle, 1974
Gelatin silver print
11 × 14 in.
Tacoma Art Museum, Gift of the artist

Signed Girl, ca. 1974
Gelatin silver print
14 × 11 in.
Tacoma Art Museum, Gift of the artist

Monroe, Washington, 1976
Gelatin silver print
10¾ × 14 in.
Tacoma Art Museum, Gift of the artist

Kane Hall, U. of W., Seattle, ca. 1998
Gelatin silver print
14 × 11 in.
Tacoma Art Museum, Gift of the artist

68 *Seattle, U. of W.,* 1998
Gelatin silver print
11 × 14 in.
Tacoma Art Museum, Gift of the artist

Francesca Sundsten
(United States, born 1960)
69 *The Crown,* 1993
Oil on canvas
19 × 19 in.
Tacoma Art Museum, Promised
gift of Dr. Jerry Slipman and
Dr. Chet Robachinski

Akio Takamori
(United States, born Japan 1950)
70 *Sleeper II,* 1998
Stoneware
11 × 28½ × 13½ in.
Tacoma Art Museum, Promised
gift of Dr. Jerry Slipman and
Dr. Chet Robachinski

Lori Talcott
(United States, born 1959)
71 *Pod Necklace,* 1999
Silver and pearls
16 × 2½ × 1 in.
Tacoma Art Museum, Anonymous gift

Sarah Ellen Taylor
(United States, born 1970)
72 *The Tarot Cards,* 2003
Etching, aquatint, and drypoint
7 × 4 in., each card
Tacoma Art Museum, Gift of
Elizabeth Ingrham

Barbara Earl Thomas
(United States, born 1948)
73 *The Storm Watch,* 1988
Egg tempera on paper
30¼ × 36 in.
Tacoma Art Museum, Gift of
Carol I. Bennett

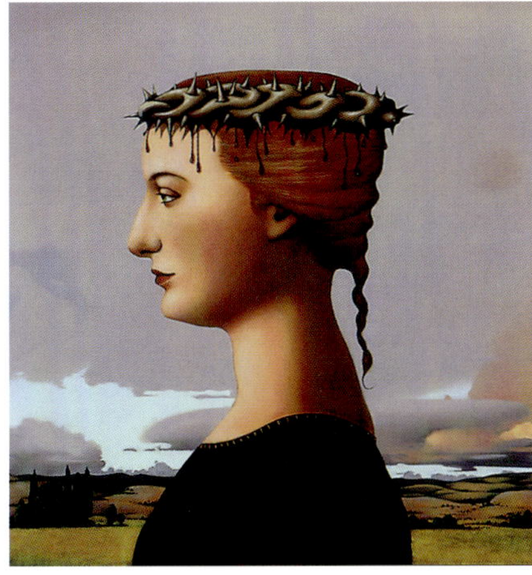

69

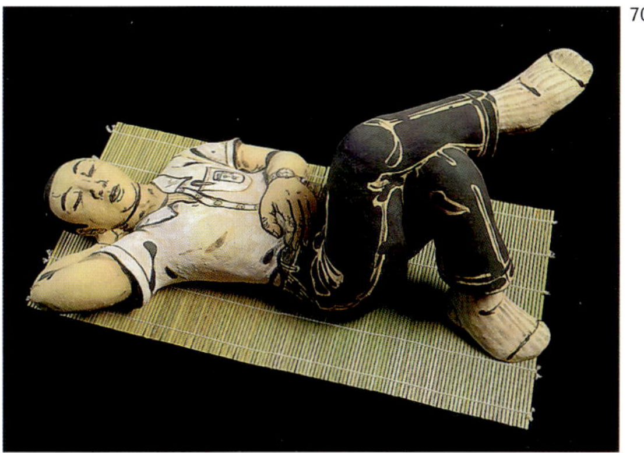

70

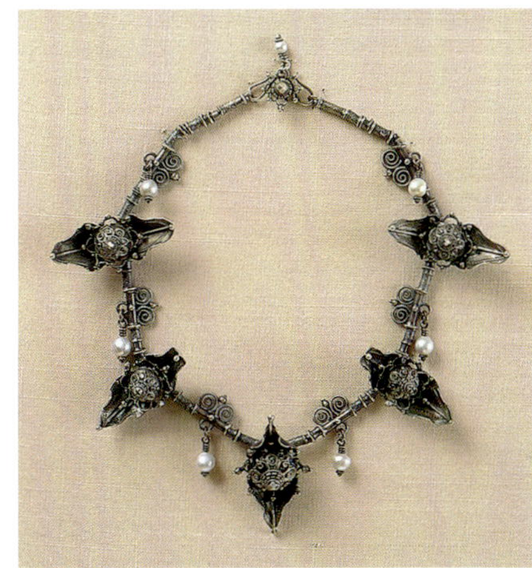

71

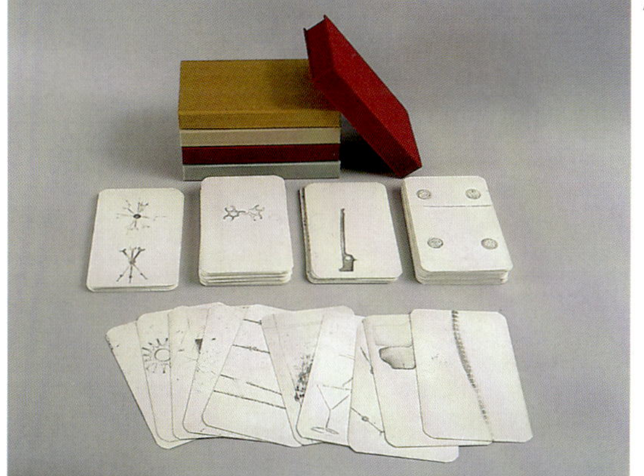

72

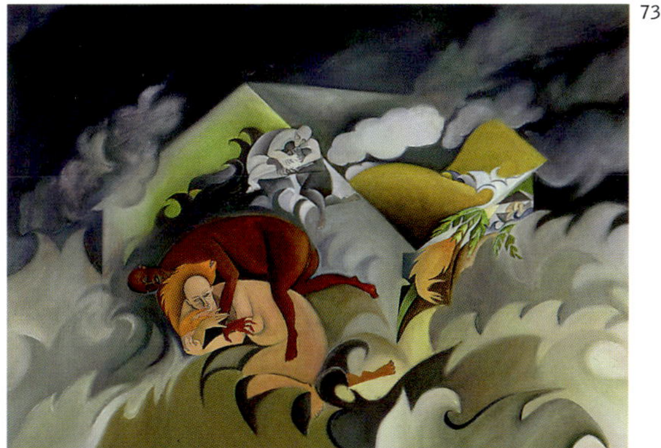

73

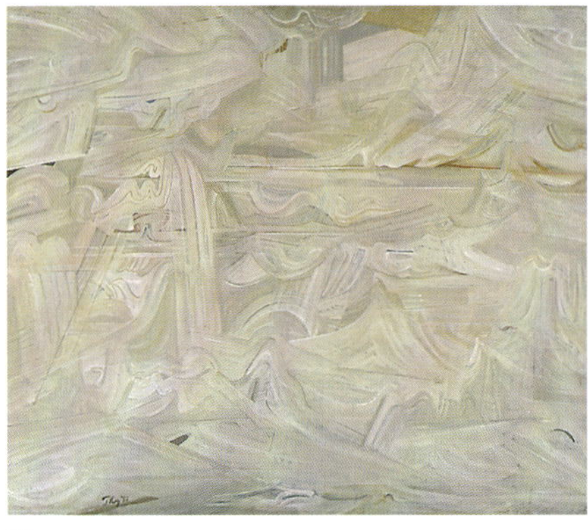

74

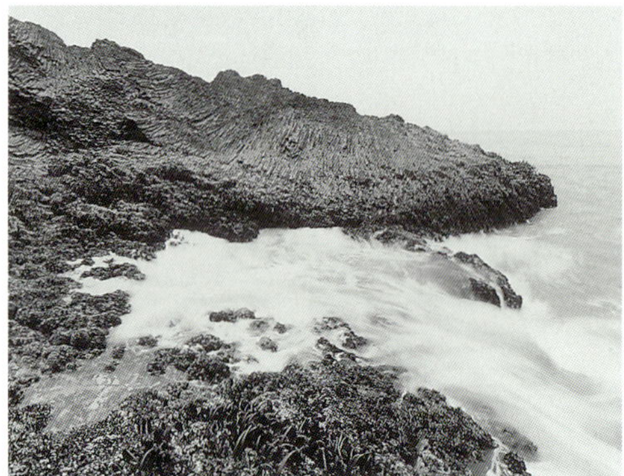

75

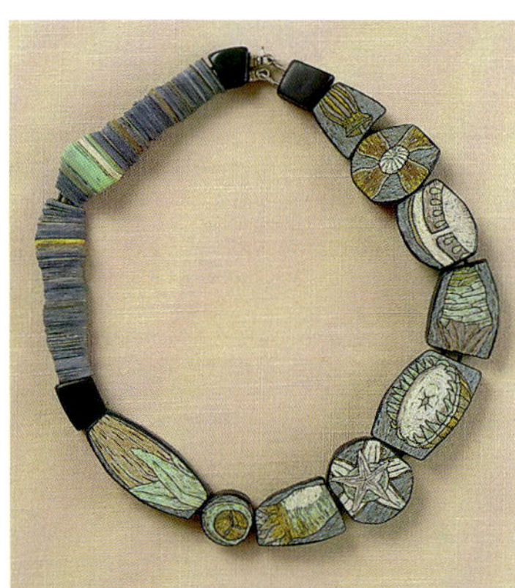

76

77

Mark Tobey
(United States, 1890–1976)
74 *Northwest Fantasy*, 1953
Tempera on paper
43 × 48½ in.
Tacoma Art Museum, Promised gift
of Anne Gould Hauberg

Terry Toedtemeier
(United States, born 1947)
Palomino Lake, Malheur Co., Oregon,
1993
Selenium-toned gelatin silver print,
no. 4 from an edition of 4
14 × 19⅞ in.
Tacoma Art Museum, Gift of the artist

Harney Desert—Oregon, 1994
Gelatin silver print
23¾ × 13⅞ in.
Tacoma Art Museum, Anonymous gift

*Serrated Edge at Big Eddy—Snake
River near Asotin, Washington,* 1995
Toned gelatin silver print, no. 2 from
an edition of 2
13⅞ × 19¾ in.
Tacoma Art Museum, Gift of the artist

*Nowhere Special—Oregon High
Desert (Probably Lake Co. or
Harney Co.),* 1997
Gelatin silver print, no. 1 from an
edition of 4
13¹⁵⁄₁₆ × 19⅞ in.
Tacoma Art Museum, Gift of the artist

*Tall Sagebrush—Coyote Trail near
Desert Lake, Lake Co., Oregon,*
ca. 1997
Gelatin silver print, no. 1 from an
edition of 5
13⅞ × 19¾ in.
Tacoma Art Museum, Gift of the artist

*Peter Looking towards the Sea—
Cavern on North Face of Cape Mears,
Tillamook Co., Oregon,* 2000
Gelatin silver print, no. 5 from an
edition of 5
20 × 16 in.
Tacoma Art Museum, Gift of the artist

*Archway in Columbia River Basalt—
North of Oceanside, Oregon,* 2001
Toned gelatin silver print
15⅞ × 19⅞ in.
Tacoma Art Museum, Gift of the artist

75 *Fanned Contraction Fractures, Cape
Foulweather, Lincoln Co., Oregon,*
2001
Toned gelatin silver print, no. 4 from
an edition of 4
16 × 20 in.
Tacoma Art Museum, Gift of the artist

*Invasive Basalt (Columbia River),
Seal Rocks State Park, Lincoln Co.,
Oregon,* 2001
Gelatin silver print
15⅞ × 20 in.
Tacoma Art Museum, Gift of the artist

*Pyramidal Rock with Bird Lime—
North of Oceanside, Oregon,* 2001
Toned gelatin silver print
15¹⁵⁄₁₆ × 19⅞ in.
Tacoma Art Museum, Gift of the artist

*Silver Point (A Remnant of a Thin Sill
in Columbia River Basalt), Clatsop
Co., Oregon,* 2001
Gelatin silver print, no. 1 from an
edition of 2
15⅞ × 19¹⁵⁄₁₆ in.
Tacoma Art Museum, Gift of the artist

Cynthia Toops
(United States, born 1956)
76 *Not Your Normal Garden Variety,
Peabody Fantasy,* 1999
Polymer clay mosaic
22 × 1½ × ½ in.
Tacoma Art Museum, Promised gift
of Donna Briskin

Molly Vidor
(United States, born 1971)
77 *Untitled (Prussian Blue),* 1999
Oil on canvas
78 × 48 in.
Tacoma Art Museum, Anonymous gift

Merrill Wagner
(United States, born 1935)
78 *Grasses,* 1997–2001
Oil pastel on slate
42 × 92 × ⅜ in.
Tacoma Art Museum, Gift of the artist

Whisk, 2001
Rust-preventative paints on steel
45 × 18 in.
Tacoma Art Museum, Gift of the artist

Marie Watt
(United States, born 1967)
79 *Omphalos,* 2002
Lithograph, no. 7 from an edition
of 12
17⅝ × 18½ in.
Tacoma Art Museum, Anonymous gift

Melissa Weinman
(United States, born 1960)
80 *ST. CLARE: Patron Saint of
Television,* 1998
Oil on canvas
60 × 36 in.
Tacoma Art Museum, Gift of the artist

Jennifer West
(United States, born 1966)
81 *Virtual Meltdown #1 (Silver Silo),*
2002
Video installation
Dimensions variable
Tacoma Art Museum, Gift of Sharon
Huling and Bill and Ruth True

Nancy Worden
(United States, born 1954)
82 *Broken Trust,* 1992
Copper, silver, malachite, garnet, onyx,
glass, and paper money
9½ × 19½ × ⅝ in.
Tacoma Art Museum, Gift of the artist

Robert Yoder
(United States, born 1962)
83 *Mather,* 2002
Painted wood
24 × 24 × 2 in.
Tacoma Art Museum, Gift of
David Lewis in honor of Garfield
and Hilda Williams

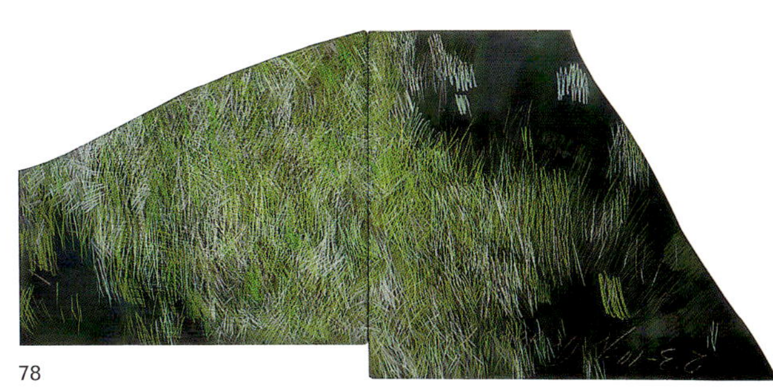

78

79

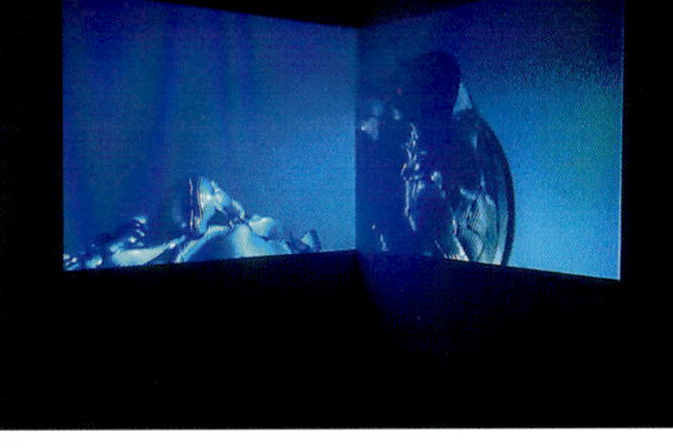

81

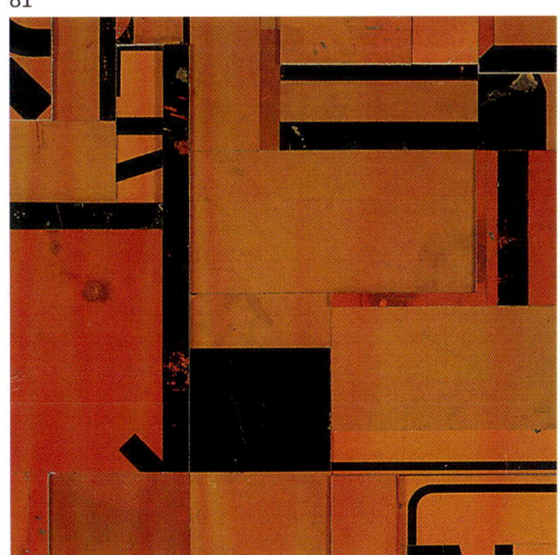

83

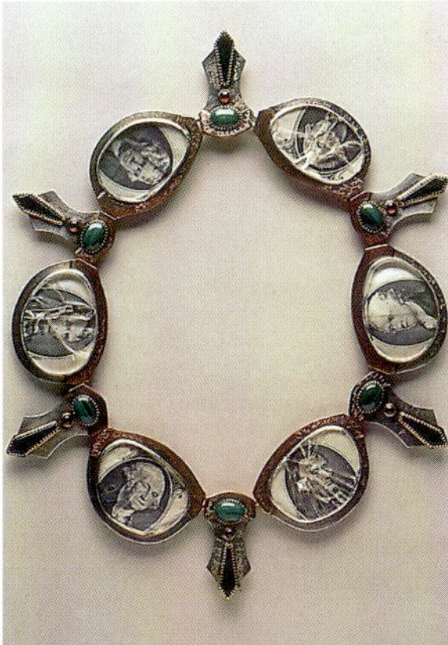

82

80

TACOMA ART MUSEUM STAFF

Janeanne A. Upp, Executive Director
Jessica Balsam, Development Assistant
Rod Bigelow, Chief Financial Officer
Derrek Bull, Security Officer
Carri Campbell, School Program Coordinator
Anna Castillo, Curator of Education
Courtenay Chamberlin, Director of
    Communications
Irene Conley, Security Officer
Sarah Dillon, Public Program Coordinator
Zoe Donnell, Curatorial Assistant
Kathe Frahm, Visitor Services
Marge Gillies, Museum Store Clerk
Kevin Guenzi, Executive Assistant
Al Haskins, Facilities Manager
Janae Huber, Registrar
Rock Hushka, Associate Curator
Sara Inveen, Manager, Individual Giving
Rebecca Jaynes, Curatorial Assistant
Jeanette Jones, Manager, Membership
    and Special Events

Robert Kane, Security Officer
Elliott Kay, Senior Accountant
Brian Kelly, Chef
Leslie Martin Kinkade, Manager, Foundation
    and Corporate Relations
Jacqueline Kosak, Registration Assistant
Maria Lautt, Visitor Services
Patricia McDonnell, Chief Curator
Arthur Navarro, Museum Store Clerk
Leslie Patton, Accounting Associate
Chelsea Perry, Public Relations Assistant
Doug Setniker, Food Service Manager
Jason Sobottka, Studio Art Coordinator
Nancy Thompson, Museum Store Manager
Katrina Townsley, Development Assistant
Vincent Warner, Preparator
Sharon Winters, Resource Center Coordinator
Tara Young, Associate Curator of Education

TACOMA ART MUSEUM
BOARD OF TRUSTEES, 2003–2004

President: Richard Carr
Vice President: Judith Nilan
Treasurer: Karen Goldstein
Secretary: Kathy McGoldrick

Lowell Buston
Karyn Clarke
Scott Cruikshank
John Dillon
Steve Finnigan
John Folsom
Dr. Shirl Gilbert
Art Grant
Susan Russell Hall
Tom Hanly
Bev Holland
Brad Jones
Alice Kaltinick
Bruce Kendall
Ottie Ladd
Bev Losey
Charles Miller
Richard Schmidtke
Dennis Seinfeld
Caryl Sherpa
Patricia Shuman
Janine Terrano
Kathryn Van Wagenen
Michael Wallingford
Jeffrey Watts

HONORARY TRUSTEES

LIFE TRUSTEES
Wendy Griffin
Alan Liddle
Dick Moe
Bill Street
Annette Weyerhaeuser

EMERITUS
Peter Darling
Esther Grant
Gene Grant
Bobby Street

NON-RESIDENT
Merrill Wagner

TACOMA ART MUSEUM
CAPITAL CAMPAIGN STEERING
COMMITTEE

Jim Griffin, Co-Chair
Wendy Griffin, Co-Chair
Carolyn Ibbotson-Woodard, Co-Chair
Ron Woodard, Co-Chair

Janet Ash
Joanne Bamford
Gretchen Bittman
Gwen Carlson
Charlotte Chalker
Peter Darling
Melanie Dressel
John Folsom
Brad Jones
Alice Kaltinick
Dawn Lucien
Martin Neeb
Mary Pascoe
Bill Street
Bobby Street
Kathryn Van Wagenen

Allen Foundation for the Arts
The Murray Foundation
City of Tacoma

The Boeing Company
Bill & Melinda Gates Foundation
Jane and George Russell
Bill and Bobby Street

Ben B. Cheney Foundation
Amy Lou Murray Eckstrom
George Davis Family
Forest Foundation
The Gottfried and Mary Fuchs Foundation
Esther and Gene Grant
Richard and Betty Hedreen
Kreielsheimer Foundation
The Kresge Foundation
M.J. Murdock Charitable Trust
The Norcliffe Foundation
Kayla Skinner
Sophie and Leslie Sussman
U.S. Department of Housing and Urban
    Development
U.S. Department of the Interior, National
    Park Service
State of Washington/Corporate Council
    for the Arts/Building for the Arts
Annette B. Weyerhaeuser
James H. and Ann R. Wiborg
Ronald Woodard and Carolyn Ibbotson-Woodard
The Bagley Wright Family Fund
Four anonymous patrons

Dr. and Mrs. Ellsworth C. Alvord, Jr.
Calvin and Joanne Bamford
Columbia Bank
Janet and Brian F. Dammeier
The Dimmer Family Foundation
John and Buzz Folsom
Frank Russell Company
Jim and Wendy Griffin
Phoebe W. Haas Charitable Trust
Erivan and Helga Haub
Sally and Philip Hayes
Microsoft Corporation
Milgard Manufacturing, Inc.
James F. and Babbie Eves Morris
Bill and Dorothy Philip
Pierce County
Pierce County Arts Commission
Mr. and Mrs. William G. Reed, Jr.
Henry T. and Shirlee A. Schatz
Peter and Janet Stanley
The Emily Hall Tremaine Foundation
U.S. Bank
Merrill Wagner
Dr. and Mrs. John Hunt Walker
Weyerhaeuser Company Foundation

Thomas and Kathryn Anderson
John L. and Anne C. Aram
Bank of America Foundation
Gweneth R. and Stanley C. Carlson
Ann and Peter Darling
Mr. and Mrs. William A. Daugherty
City of Fife
Gordon, Thomas, Honeywell, Malanca,
    Peterson & Daheim, PLLC
Mrs. Charles J. Gould
Rod and LaVerne Hagenbuch
Anne Gould Hauberg
The Hyde Foundation
Paul R. and Alice Kaltinick
Florence B. Kilworth Foundation
William W. Kilworth Foundation
Larry and Judith Kopp
Ottie and Clara Ladd
City of Lakewood
Chauncey and Elizabeth Lufkin
Macdonald Building Company, LLC
Moccasin Lake Foundation
Dick and Marcia Moe
National Endowment for the Arts
The News Tribune
Jon and Mary Shirley
Phil and Snookey Simon
Stone McLaren
Titcomb Foundation
Michael A. Tucci Family
Marylu and Peter Wallerich
C. Davis Weyerhaeuser
Mr. and Mrs. George H. Weyerhaeuser
Lynn Weyerhaeuser and Stanley Ray Day Fund
Judy and John Woodworth